His mother, _____ _____ e world's most beloved icon of all time. His father is the Prince of Wales, heir to the British throne. His grandmother, the queen of England herself.

Here, for the first time, is an in-depth account of the life of a boy who might not have been born to be king—but whose extraordinary circumstances have placed him squarely from the moment of his birth in the unrelenting glare of the media.

What makes Prince Harry tick? Who is the real person behind those endearing boy-next-door looks: the shock of red hair, upturned nose, and impish grin? How has he dealt with the blows of the past few years, from his parents' divorce to his mother's tragic death? What's it like to be kid brother to the future king? What will the prince look for in a girl when it comes time to choose his future wife?

The answers to these questions and many, many more lie in the pages ahead—required reading for anyone who's joined the rapidly expanding ranks of those who are absolutely, positively wild about Harry!

BOOK YOUR PLACE ON OUR WEBSITE AND MAKE THE READING CONNECTION!

We've created a customized website just for our very special readers, where you can get the inside scoop on everything that's going on with Zebra, Pinnacle and Kensington books.

When you come online, you'll have the exciting opportunity to:

- View covers of upcoming books
- Read sample chapters
- Learn about our future publishing schedule (listed by publication month *and author*)
- Find out when your favorite authors will be visiting a city near you
- Search for and order backlist books from our online catalog
- Check out author bios and background information
- Send e-mail to your favorite authors
- Meet the Kensington staff online
- Join us in weekly chats with authors, readers and other guests
- Get writing guidelines
- AND MUCH MORE!

**Visit our website at
http://www.pinnaclebooks.com**

PRINCE
HARRY

Wendy Brody

PINNACLE BOOKS
KENSINGTON PUBLISHING CORP
www.pinnaclebooks.com

PINNACLE BOOKS are published by

Kensington Publishing Corp.
850 Third Avenue
New York, NY 10022

All Kensington Titles, Imprints, and Distributed Lines are available at special quantity discounts for bulk purchases for sales promotions, premiums, fund-raising, educational, or institutional use. Special book excerpts or customized printings can also be created to fit specific needs. For details, write or phone the office of the Kensington special sales manager: Kensington Publishing Corp., 850 Third Avenue, New York, NY 10022, attn: Special Sales Department, Phone: 1-800-221-2647

First Printing: September, 2000
10 9 8 7 6 5 4 3 2 1

Printed in the United States of America

As always, to Mark and Morgan.

*But this time, most of all, to my own sweet, pint-size
second son, Brody,
who, like Prince Harry, is a gutsy, happy-go-lucky
charmer!*

ACKNOWLEDGMENTS

The author would like to thank the following people for their help with the research for this book: Tom Staub, Nicole Watson, Bree Neely, Nicole Hermatz, Rosanna Chiofolo, John Scognamiglio, Elisabeth Weed, Fran Collier, R. Stevan Jonas, Patty Karmen, Molly Carew, Suzanne Staub, Reg Corsi, Fran Corsi, Meryl Nelson, David Staub, Lucia Macro, and Felicia Staub.

Also, thank you to Debby Benz and Van Kozelka at the Katonah Village Library. Your patience and time-consuming assistance was greatly appreciated!

ACKNOWLEDGMENTS

Contents

Introduction

His mother was arguably the world's most beloved icon of all time. His father is the Prince of Wales, heir to the British Throne. His grandmother, the queen of England herself.

But what about His Royal Highness (HRH) Prince Henry Charles Albert David Windsor, better known as simply "Harry"?

"He's super cute, seemingly outgoing, funny, plays my favorite sports, cute, is normal, and did I mention cute? Well, he is." So declares a smitten female named Beverly on one of the many Internet Web sites devoted to the younger son of Prince Charles and the late princess Diana.

A heartthrob in his own right, Prince Harry has nonetheless—and quite predictably—been overshadowed by his enormously popular elder brother, Prince William. Dubbed at birth "the

Spare"—as in "the Heir and the Spare"—Harry has indeed been spared the daunting weight that rests squarely on William's shoulders: nothing less than the future of the British monarchy itself. Third in line for the throne, he is unlikely to ascend. That means his life, unlike his brother's, will largely be led on his own terms—to the extent that is, that a royal can live his own life.

What does the future hold for Harry? That's anyone's guess.

As for his past . . .

Here, for the first time, is an in-depth account of the life of a boy who might not have been born to be king—but whose extraordinary circumstances have placed him squarely in the unrelenting glare of the media from the moment of his birth, the news of which appeared on the front page of the *New York Times*.

What makes Prince Harry tick? Who is the real person behind those endearing boy-next-door looks: the shock of red hair, upturned nose, and impish grin? How has he dealt with the blows of the past few years, from his parents' divorce to his mother's tragic death? What's it like to be kid brother to the future king? What will the prince look for in a girl when it comes time to choose his future wife?

The answers to these questions and many, many more lie in the pages ahead—required reading for anyone who's joined the rapidly expanding ranks of those who are absolutely, positively wild about Harry!

Fast Facts

Full Name: His Royal Highness (HRH) Prince Henry Charles Albert David Windsor

Nickname: Prince Harry

Birth Date: September 15, 1984

Birthplace: St. Mary's Hospital, Paddington, London

Parents: Prince Charles and Princess Diana

Siblings: His Royal Highness Prince William Arthur Philip Louis, a.k.a. "Wills"

First Home: Kensington Palace, London

Hair Color: red

Eye Color: blue

Education: Mrs. Mynor's Nursery School, Wetherby School, Ludgrove School, Eton College

---

CHAPTER I

The Royal Family

On July 29, 1981, the entire world—well, *almost*: an estimated 750 million people in more than seventy countries around the globe—watched as Britain's Prince Charles married Lady Diana Frances Spencer at St. Paul's Cathedral in London.

To a city steeped in unemployment, and for a monarchy whose glory days seemed to be long over, the royal wedding was a fairy-tale dream come true—perhaps for everyone, but the bride and groom.

The third daughter of a rich earl, whose family had made its fortunes centuries earlier as sheep traders, Diana had grown up wanting for very little in terms of material things. Born July 1, 1961, and raised at Park House, the Norfolk mansion presented to her maternal grandfather by King

George V, and at Althorp, the vast Spencer family estate, she was surrounded by the trappings of great European wealth. The well-connected Spencers rubbed shoulders with the cream of British aristocracy—including the royal family, whose Sandringham estate was directly next door to Park House.

But as the product of a broken home, Diana endured a lonely childhood. Her two older sisters, Sarah and Jane, were already at boarding school by the time she arrived. It was no secret that Diana's father, Viscount Althorp, desperately longed for a male heir. Disappointed when his wife, Frances, bore him two daughters, he was elated when the third Spencer child turned out to be a son, John—and devastated when the baby died hours later.

Eighteen months later, Diana came along. Her gender caused her parents such shock and dismay that it took them a week to come up with a girl's name. Her brother, Charles, the male heir who was finally born three years after Diana, later attributed his parents' frustration over the birth of their third daughter as one of the causes of their divorce.

Though Diana must have resented her kid brother for claiming the parental spotlight, as well as the Spencer legacy and fortune, Charles was her closest childhood companion. Seized by a keen maternal instinct she would later display with her own sons, Diana comforted and took care of her brother after their parents split when Diana was six and Charles only three.

There's no question that the divorce was traumatic for them. Although their mother sued their father for custody of the children, Diana and her siblings were awarded to their father. Their mother's case wasn't helped by the fact that she'd left her husband for another man, Peter Shand Kydd, whom she later married.

When she wasn't away at boarding school herself, shy Diana spent her childhood in the care of nannies, some of them abusive, others kindly mother-figures—but none an adequate substitute for the constant loving nurture of her own mum.

As a little girl craving maternal attention and affection, she may have vowed that when she grew up and had children of her own, she would be there for them in a way that her own mother hadn't been for her.

Prince Charles could no doubt relate to Diana's overprivileged but sadly neglected youth. While his parents' marriage survived more than five decades of public scrutiny, the relationship between Queen Elizabeth and Prince Philip wasn't the warmest in the world, and the Windsors' family life was anything but cozy when Charles was a boy. His mother raised him in the royal tradition—that is, she was consumed by royal duties and travel, leaving her children in the care of nannies who witnessed the milestones she missed: the children's first teeth, their first steps.

Aside from photo ops that were carefully engineered to create an image of Elizabeth as a doting mother, she rarely spent time with Charles, his younger sister, Anne, or his brothers, Andrew and Edward, as they were growing up.

The royal family isn't exactly known as an affectionate bunch, either. When Harry's grandfather Prince Philip gave the queen a chaste, public kiss on the cheek—their first in the history of their marriage—at midnight on the millennial New Year's Eve 2000, the landmark event made the press.

Tutored at home until he was eight, Charles was the first royal heir sent away to boarding school, at the insistence of his father, whom he idolized. The young prince attended his father's alma maters: first Cheam School, a rigorous prep academy, then Scotland's grueling Gordonstoun School, where he was miserable—and hardly a star pupil. Eton College, where William and Harry would later be educated, was ruled out.

At Trinity College in Cambridge in the late 1960s, a young Charles pretty much ignored the hippie scene that was embraced by his generation. Straitlaced and sensible, he played polo and skied, and like any fine country nobleman, was interested in hunting, fishing, and gardening.

Women flocked around him, and he overcame his initial shy awkwardness to become the world's most eligible bachelor. Eventually, he embarked—perhaps against his will—on a search for a suitable bride, a quest that would last more than a decade.

One of the prince's first—and maybe his only true—loves was his friend Camilla Shand. Charles became involved with the hardy, outgoing daughter of a wealthy wine merchant while he was in his early twenties, and rekindled the relationship after her marriage to Andrew Parker Bowles. Although they shared a passion for the outdoors, and—as she pointed out when they first met—her great-grandmother had been his great-great grandfather's lover, Charles and Camilla weren't meant to be. At least, not back then.

His duty to his country had to come before any personal preference. Charles was destined to marry and produce an heir to the throne. By the time he reached his early thirties, he was under constant pressure by his parents, the royal advisors, and the press to get on with it.

It wasn't as if he could marry strictly for love, either. His bride would have to be a well-bred aristocrat, Protestant, able to bear children, and—perhaps most importantly—have spotless virtue.

Twelve years younger than the future king, pretty, blond Lady Diana Spencer fit the bill. She was literally the girl next door, with her home, Park House, sharing a property border with the royal estate.

In fact, it was at Sandringham that they had first met during a holiday celebration, when Diana was a child and Charles a grown man. They ran into each other again when she was in her teens and he was a sought-after bachelor dating her sister Sarah. Then, on a fateful afternoon in July 1980, they wound up sitting next to each other on a hayride at the home of mutual friends in West Sussex.

At that point, Diana was sharing a London flat with three friends and working several jobs, one at the Young England kindergarten, another as a house cleaner, another as part-time nanny for an American family living abroad. She wholeheartedly adored children, but was forced to give up her work with them when her romance with Prince Charles landed her in international headlines.

On February 6, 1981, Diana accepted Charles's marriage proposal. She was in love with him and excited about their future together, although she had her anxieties, too. She knew her life was about to change forever.

Meanwhile, when the engagement was announced to the press a few weeks later, Charles hedged when reporters asked him if he was in love with her. He reluctantly agreed that he was, "whatever love means."

Diana must have been stung, but it didn't show. This was the first of many, many times that she would be forced to conceal her true feelings and publicly put on a brave face.

In the months leading up to the royal wedding, Diana, who had moved into Buckingham Palace the night before the engagement became public, was hounded by the media. She ducked her head—charmingly, many thought—in the cameras' glare, and soon was bestowed with the nickname "Shy Di."

Charles, used to being the center of attention, was taken aback at the way his future bride had stolen the spotlight. Although he publicly acted as though he found the media's defection amusing, in years to come his resentment of the way his wife upstaged him would reportedly contribute to the troubled marriage's ultimate failure.

So would Diana's secret illness. Always insecure with her self-image, she fell victim to a fierce eating disorder in the months leading up to her marriage. Under the intense media scrutiny, the slightly plump girl, now known around the world as "Shy Di," shrunk several dress sizes and became a fashion icon. The newly lean princess began to cultivate a classic style and a glamorous image that belied the agony of the disease that was ravaging her. She even managed to conceal her bulimia from her fiancé, who didn't discover the truth until they were on their honeymoon.

Aboard the royal yacht *Britannia*, the newlyweds cruised the Mediterranean sea—accompanied by nearly three hundred sailors, including a Royal Marine band. Not exactly an idyllic getaway for two!

Diana must have felt disillusioned when her husband showed more interest in reading and fishing than in romancing his new bride. In fact, she later admitted that it was during their honeymoon that she learned of her husband's continuing affair with Camilla Parker Bowles.

The prince and princess spent that August, September, and October at Balmoral, the queen's estate in the Scottish Highlands. During this time, Diana battled her illness, struggled to come to terms with marriage to a man who loved another woman, and did her best to adjust to the strangeness of life within the royal family.

She also became pregnant.

Her life now a series of official engagements, flashing cameras, and tabloid headlines, the princess was deathly ill with morning sickness. Yet she and Charles were thrilled about the prospect of parenthood. Maybe they both believed the birth of a child could save a marriage that was in trouble from the very start.

About a month before Diana gave birth, she and Charles moved from London's Buckingham Palace to nearby Kensington Palace, which they shared with other royals such as Princess Margaret, the queen's younger sister. On weekends they visited their 353-acre country estate, Highgrove, in Gloucestershire. Diana, known for her sense of style and color, when it came to fashion, now took on a new challenge, playing a large role in decorating both homes—with professional help, of course.

His Royal Highness Prince William Arthur Philip Louis Windsor was born at St. Mary's Hospital to great fanfare on June 21, 1982—the first royal baby to be born in a hospital rather than in the palace. With his birth, the future of the monarchy was secure for another generation— and Diana was the nation's heroine.

History repeated itself when Diana and Charles, like her parents before them, took several days to name their new baby. Charles admitted they were arguing about names. It wasn't the first time they would disagree where their children were concerned.

Charles had a heavy hand in choosing the godparents, who included royalty and titled dignitaries instead of close friends and family, as Diana probably would have preferred. They included Princess Alexandra; the Duchess of Westminster; Lady Susan Hussey; King Constantine II of the Hellenes; Lord Romsey; and Sir Laurens Van der Post.

Diana was determined to be the kind of mother she had never had—a mother who lavished her children with hugs and kisses. She vowed that her royal children would live as "normal" a life as possible.

Still, she obviously couldn't hang around the nursery all day. She had countless official duties to fulfill—which meant she would have to hire a nanny. Barbara Barnes was her name.

Though Prince William was in the nanny's care much of the time, both his parents reportedly changed plenty of diapers and bathed their son themselves. Charles appeared to be a more "hands-on" parent than Elizabeth or Philip had been, and Diana was utterly devoted to her baby.

But the little family wasn't exactly living in a storybook world. Any new parents will wholeheartedly say that it isn't easy to adjust to having a child. For this famous pair, the transition was especially hard. Not only was their every move watched—and often criticized—by people around the globe, but Diana's bulimia tormented her, and Charles wasn't emotionally equipped to deal with her problems.

Add to this their high-pressure royal duties, and the fact that he still had a bond with Camilla Parker Bowles—something a heartbroken Diana knew. Later, in her famed televised interview with the BBC, she would candidly say, "There were three of us in this marriage, so it was a bit crowded."

But as stressful as those first years of the marriage were, they weren't without their happy moments. As a difficult 1983 drew to a close, giving way to brighter hopes for 1984, Diana discovered she was pregnant again.

This time, although she again suffered with morning sickness, and still had to maintain a frantic, high-profile schedule, Diana at least knew what to expect. That undoubtedly made the pregnancy a bit less traumatic—although something else made it difficult in another way.

According to Andrew Morton's book *Diana: Her True Story*—a biographical account that was written with the princess's admitted cooperation—Prince Charles fervently wanted their second child to be a girl.

Imagine how Diana felt when she learned from an ultrasound in the months before Harry's birth that she was carrying another boy. After all, her own father had longed for a son and was bitterly disappointed when Diana, his third daughter, entered the world.

She must have felt a certain kinship with Harry even before he was born—and most likely vowed that her second son would never sense his father's disappointment, as she had so acutely felt the earl's.

Diana kept the knowledge of her unborn baby's sex to herself that summer of 1984. Her pregnancy had been made public that spring, just before Prince William's second birthday in June. The kingdom rejoiced at the news that another royal heir was imminent.

Diana visited Harrods, one of London's finest department stores, and picked out a layette for the baby. William's hand-me-downs wouldn't do—after all, the new baby would be a prince or princess, too! So she bought new towels, a new crib, and a whole new wardrobe for the baby, whose due date was estimated at September 22.

On July 1, Diana's twenty-third birthday, she went to a polo match in Gloucestershire. It was supposed to be a happy outing, but tragedy struck when a woman approaching the royal box to greet Diana was trampled to death by a pony. The pregnant princess was horrified and deeply shaken by the accident.

Yet once she had gotten past the trauma, it became a happy, expectant summer. William, no longer an infant, delighted his parents as he toddled cheerfully around. Now that the strain of having a newborn was far behind them, the members of the young family had settled into their roles and seemed to enjoy one another.

Diana would later say that during this period she and Charles were closer than ever. With the usual pressure of her official schedule temporarily relieved due to her pregnancy, Diana spent much of the summer in seclusion at Highgrove in Gloucestershire.

In August she went as usual with Charles and William to Balmoral, the royal family's Scottish retreat. But her days there were marred by the news that her favorite uncle, Lord Fermoy, had committed suicide on the grounds of his sprawling manor near the royal estate at Sandringham. Weeping, Diana traveled alone to the funeral, wearing a black silk maternity dress.

Finally, as the weather turned crisp and the official start of autumn loomed just days ahead, a smiling, expectant Princess Diana—cheerily clad in red—returned to St. Mary's Hospital in Paddington, located in a relatively downscale neighborhood in the northern part of London. The trip took about thirty minutes by car from Kensington Palace, and Diana reached the hospital by around seven A.M.

There, in the Lindo Wing—the private section where she'd delivered her first child—she entered a $175-a-day, twelve-foot-by-twelve-foot room that, like many delivery rooms in hospitals around the world, was starkly furnished with a bed, an armchair, and a television set.

As morning gave way to midday, Princess Diana went through nine hours of labor. During the early stages she was able to relax somewhat and read a paperback novel, with Prince Charles dozing in a bedside armchair.

By around one o'clock, though, things had become grueling. A determined baby was fighting his way into the world, intent on making his debut a full week before his due date.

Outside the hospital, a huge crowd had gathered—no smaller than the throng that had awaited William's birth a little over two years earlier. In addition to the kingdom's loyal subjects, there were more than three hundred reporters from around the world, news vans, TV technicians, and dozens of police officers to keep everyone under control.

Diana was determined to get through the birth without drugs, concerned for the baby's well-being. As her labor intensified, she sucked on ice cubes to prevent dehydration. Charles, clad in a green hospital gown and surgical mask, stayed at her side, along with the nurses and the royal gynecologist, Dr. George Pinker.

Finally, as the late-afternoon sky outside Diana's window began to darken, threatening both evening and rain, the exhausted princess bore down triumphantly, and a baby's first lusty cries pierced the air.

The USA When Harry Was Born

On Saturday, September 15, 1984, the *New York Times* contained headlines about the American presidential election, contract disputes at the United Auto Workers union, that evening's Miss America pageant in Atlantic City, and the ironically named Hurricane Diana, which had pummeled the North Carolina coast for three days.

One of the esteemed paper's front-page captions on the following day would read "A boy for the princess" and an inside story would be headlined "PRINCESS OF WALES GIVES BIRTH TO HER SECOND SON."

Prince Harry was born in a year that had been immortalized long before it dawned, in George Orwell's futuristic novel *1984* (which had been written three and a half decades earlier). Although Orwell foresaw a monochromatic London where people's actions were eerily monitored by Big Brother and their minds by Thought Police, newborn

Harry's world thankfully bore little resemblance.

It was a world in which rap and hip-hop, hugely popular today, were still largely confined to the ghetto streets, although the first all-rap radio format was introduced that year by KDAY in Los Angeles.

Scandals were rampant: Sydney Biddle Barrows, a.k.a. the Mayflower Madam, was busted for running a high-profile call-girl ring and later capitalized on her fame by writing a best-selling book. Nude photos of Vanessa Williams, the reigning Miss America, forced her to give up her crown to the first runner-up, Suzette Charles. (In the annual pageant held the very night Harry was born, she in turn passed her crown to Miss Utah, Sharlene Wells.) Vanessa Williams went on to become a successful recording artist.

Former first lady Betty Ford went public with her alcoholism, paving the way for the more open treatment and admission of celebrities' problems and addictions that would evolve in years to come. Medical history was made when a baboon's heart was successfully transplanted into a human known only as Baby Faye. Political turmoil was rampant around the globe: Russian leader Yri Andropov died that February and was replaced by Konstantin Chernenko, and Indira Gandhi was assassinated less than two weeks before Harry was born.

By the time the young prince reached his teens, Sarajevo, Yugoslavia, would be consumed by the horrors of war. Yet in the winter of 1984, the world closely watched Sarajevo for a very different reason: the city hosted the Winter Olympics. There, figure skaters Katarina Witt and Scott Hamilton were notable gold medalists. That summer, as Diana and Charles were preparing their nursery for their second child, the Olympics were hosted in Los Angeles. Track-and-field competitor Carl Lewis and gymnast Mary Lou Retton were among the medalists who emerged from obscurity that summer to become household names. And gold-medalist diver Greg Louganis would later make waves with his memoir *Breaking the Surface*, in which he revealed he had AIDS.

It was an election year in the United States, with President Ronald Reagan and Vice President George Bush, Republicans, running against Democratic challengers Walter Mondale and his vice presidential candidate, Geraldine Ferraro, the first female ever to run on a major party's presidential ticket. Reagan and Bush would win by a landslide that November.

The top-grossing movie that year was *Ghostbusters;* the number-one American television show was *Dynasty. The Cosby Show,* which would go on to become one of the most popular sitcoms of all time, made its first appearance the month Harry was born.

Here's some additional entertainment and sports information that further captures the world in the year of 1984:

At the Movies: *Indiana Jones and the Temple of Doom, Beverly Hills Cop, Gremlins, The Woman in Red, The Karate Kid*

Film Stars: Harrison Ford, Sally Field, Bill Murray, Meryl Streep, Eddie Murphy, Kathleen Turner, Clint Eastwood, Richard Gere

On Television: *Newhart; Kate & Allie; Family Ties; Dynasty; Hill Street Blues; Miami Vice; Cagney & Lacey; St. Elsewhere; Night Court; Murder, She Wrote; Cheers; Magnum, P.I.; Dallas*

Best-selling Books: *The Talisman* (Stephen King and Peter Straub), *Iacoca* (Lee Iacoca)

Recording Artists: Michael Jackson, Bruce Springsteen, Tina Turner, Lionel Richie, Phil Collins, Cyndi Lauper, Prince

Heisman Trophy Winner: Doug Flutie

Superbowl XVIII: Los Angeles Raiders beat Washington Redskins

World Series: Detroit Tigers beat San Diego Padres

Wimbledon: Martina Navratilova won Women's Singles; John McEnroe won Men's Singles

CHAPTER 2

Birth of a Prince

His Royal Highness Prince Henry Charles Albert
David of Wales entered the world at 4:20 P.M. that
Saturday afternoon, September 15, 1984. The
bouncing baby boy, with light blue eyes and a bit
of reddish fuzz on his head, weighed six pounds,
fourteen ounces.

Outside the hospital, town crier Julian Shepherd, clad in traditional red uniform, ceremoniously rang a bell and announced the joyful
tidings.

Bedlam ensued. The mob roared. Church bells
chimed. Champagne corks popped. A traditional
forty-one gun salute was fired from the Tower of
London; another in Hyde Park by the Queen's
Troop, the Royal Horse Artillery. And a driver
passing the hospital was so overcome by the

news that he plowed his car into the side of an ambulance.

The throngs that had gathered were simply ecstatic at the news that a new prince had been born—as, presumably, the rest of the royal family was when Charles telephoned them at the Balmoral estate to relay the newest Windsor's vital statistics. Now the monarchy had its heir, Prince William, and its "spare," Prince Harry, who would take over the throne if for any reason his brother couldn't.

An official bulletin was promptly posted at the Highlands castle. It read simply: "Her Royal Highness the Princess of Wales was safely delivered of a son at 4:20 P.M. today. Her Royal Highness and the child are both well."

Meanwhile, at Althorp in Northhampton, Diana's delighted father commemorated the occasion by raising the family flag. He informed the press, "All went very well . . . I think the person who will be very pleased will be Prince William, because it will be wonderful for him to have a little companion and a playmate . . . and someone to fight with . . . I'm sure Harry will be a very good chap."

It's been widely said that Charles was disappointed when his second child wasn't the daughter he longed for. According to Andrew Morton's *Diana: Her True Story*, a biography that relied heavily on input from Diana herself, Charles merely said, "Oh, it's a boy . . . and he's even got rusty hair."

But he appeared beaming and proud when he greeted the public and press outside the hospital early that evening. He reported that the newborn was "absolutely marvelous. It didn't matter whether it was a boy or girl. . . . We have nearly got a full polo team now. . . . My wife is very well. The delivery couldn't have been better. It was much quicker this time than last time."

The moment Harry's birth was announced, bookmakers started taking bets on what his parents would name him. The odds were in favor of George (after Queen Elizabeth's father, King George VI), followed by Philip (after his paternal grandfather). This time, Charles and Diana waited less than twenty-four hours to name their son. Buckingham Palace announced on Sunday, September 16, that the little prince would be christened Henry Charles Albert David.

Henry is a popular name with royals, dating back to the twelfth century and King Henry I, the son of William the Conqueror. It was Henry II who ordered the murder of Thomas à Becket in Canterbury Cathedral. In 1598 Henry IV signed the Edict of Nantes granting religious freedom to Protestant Hughenots. Henry V, famed for his 1415 victory over the French at the Battle of

Agincourt and 1420 capture of Paris, was immortalized by Shakespeare. And the sixteenth century's colorful, much-married King Henry VIII—two of his unfaithful wives, including Anne Boleyn, were beheaded—was probably the most famous British monarch of all time, so much so that he was immortalized in a catchy Herman's Hermits pop tune in the 1960s.

According to Buckingham Palace, the infant's second name, Charles, was chosen to honor not just his father, but also the Spencer family (Diana's brother, Harry's uncle, the Earl Spencer, is also Charles). The palace attributed the name Albert to Prince Charles's grandfather, George VI, and to Queen Victoria's husband, and the name David to the Queen Mother's late brother, David Bowes Lyon.

The palace also announced the newborn child would be known as just "Harry" at home.

Harry's first official visitor was his two-year-old big brother, who showed up at the hospital in a Mercedes station wagon with Charles and his nanny to visit his day-old sibling. Wills showed no sign of the jealousy that's so typical of older kids upon the birth of a new baby. Instead, he smothered little Harry with affection, patting him and holding his hand, and instantly established a solid bond that has clearly lasted from that first precious day forward.

Harry met his public when he was only thirteen hours old. As his mother appeared outside the hospital, beaming and protectively clutching a blanketed bundle, the crowds that had been there all night erupted into cheers, shouting, "Hurrah, Harry!"

Diana looked radiant. Her blond hair was perfectly coiffed, her face made-up and bearing no signs of the utter exhaustion she must have felt. She wore a smart red suit with a red-and-white-striped blouse, fashionably tied at the neckline. Charles, clad in a dark suit and tie, was at her side, beaming as the photographers snapped away.

Mother and child lingered in the hospital only twenty-two hours after Saturday's birth. Diana was eager to get home and enjoy her new baby in the quiet yellow-and-white nursery, with its painted bunny murals and comfortable antique furniture. The worn-out new mom longed to get away from the glare of the spotlight, to be safe in her little nest with her baby at her side. Charles, on the other hand, reportedly didn't stick around to change Harry's diapers on that first afternoon under their own roof. Instead, he drove off in his Aston Martin to play polo—and was promptly criticized in the press.

From that point on, the marriage of Diana and Charles seemed to undergo a significant transition. While they had expertly hidden the strain in the years leading up to Harry's birth, it now became increasingly obvious to the world that the Prince and Princess of Wales weren't living happily ever after. Diana would later admit that Harry's birth marked the end of their marriage. But another decade would pass before they would officially do something about it.

Like William, Harry was bombarded with flowers, balloons, telegrams, and gifts from around the world, perhaps most notably a miniature antique piano from the American singer Barry Manilow.

Soon Harry settled into the palace nursery, breast-fed every three hours by his indulgent mother and watched over by diligent nannies. Barbara Barnes was assisted by Olga Powell, who was in her late fifties and a bit more strict than the doting Nanny Barnes.

Of course, Harry also had his own "detectives," or security guards, who were assigned to all members of the royal family.

After all, his aunt, Princess Anne—like Harry, a second-born royal child—was nearly kidnapped in 1974, when a gunman accosted her limo outside of Buckingham Palace. And his great-great uncle, Lord Mountbatten, was killed with other members of his family by an IRA terrorist bomb in 1979.

Sheltered as newborn Harry's world was, the

threat that somebody might try to harm one of the royals was ever present.

When the time came to choose Harry's god-parents, there was speculation that the eighty-six-year-old American millionaire tycoon Armand Hammer would be chosen out of respect for his friendship with Charles. It didn't happen.

The list once again included British nobility, al-though Harry's father seems to have bent to his wife's wishes more than he had the first time around. Diana's close friend and former room-mate Carolyn Pride Bartholomew was chosen as a godmother, along with Celia (Cece), Lady Vestey; and Lady Sarah Armstrong-Jones, the daughter of the queen's sister, Princess Margaret. Harry's godfathers are polo player Gerald Ward, artist Bryan Organ, and Charles's younger brother Prince Andrew.

According to author Kitty Kelley's book *The Royals*, Diana refused to ask Charles's sister, Princess Anne, to be Harry's godmother. While the sisters-in-law were civil, they reportedly couldn't stand each other. Prince Philip, who had always outwardly favored Anne over her three brothers, was furious when she wasn't invited to christen her new nephew.

As a result, Kelley says, Philip didn't visit his new grandson for six weeks—and a miffed Anne boycotted the christening.

Meanwhile, Diana's father, the Earl Spencer, took a special interest in his second grandson. Concerned, as Diana was, that Harry, unlike William, wasn't going to inherit the kingdom—and the massive fortune that went with it—the earl invested roughly $1 million for Harry, hoping to secure his future (not that he was a doting grandfather who regularly saw his royal grandsons or had a major role in their upbringing).

Diana didn't get along with her father's second wife, Raine, whom he had married in 1976, when his youngest daughter was still a teenager. Her stepmother, the daughter of famed romance novelist Barbara Cartland, was a flamboyant woman who, to put it kindly, appreciated the esteemed Spencer name and all that accompanied it.

Diana and her siblings, who called her "acid rain," resented their father's new wife's intrusion on their lives and the changes she made at Althrop. They barely tolerated her on the rare occasions when the family was together, although in later years, Diana seemed to have at least attempted to make some amends.

Harry's birth triggered a souvenir industry worth $25 million, complete with commemorative mugs, thimbles, and china dolls. Yet Diana was, even before the baby was born, aware that he was in danger of developing an inferiority complex. Determined to see that he wasn't overlooked, she was in tune with his needs from the start.

At the time of his birth she said, "Royal first-borns may get all the glory, but second borns enjoy more freedom. . . . only when Harry is a lot older will he realize how lucky he is not to have been the eldest. My second child will never have quite the same sort of pressure that poor William must face all his life."

By the time Harry was five weeks old, he weighed eight pounds, ten ounces, and was ready to sit for his first official family portrait. He wore a white cotton gown with lace edging at the sleeves, and his great-uncle Lord Snowdon photographed the event at Kensington Palace.

One photograph shows William cradling Harry on his lap, both of the little princes barefoot and appearing totally relaxed with each other. In fact, sleepy Harry was so secure and contented in his big brother's arms that he closed his eyes and yawned!

However, William, who delighted in climbing into and out of Harry's bed to be close to his brother, wasn't always gentle with him. The enthusiastic older sibling occasionally had to be restrained from overzealously hugging and kissing his baby brother.

At three months of age, Harry was christened by the Archbishop of Canterbury on December

21, 1984, at Windsor Castle, in St. George's Chapel. He wore an enormous, old-fashioned cream-colored, lace-trimmed christening gown that billowed from his mother's arms as she cuddled him close.

Television cameras were there to mark the landmark event. They also captured Harry's headstrong big brother William acting up after being told he couldn't hold Harry, as he loved so much to do.

This public evidence that William—or Wills, as the family called him—was in the throes of the "terrible twos" caused quite a stir in the press—and within the royal family. In particular, William's grandmother, the queen, was most displeased. While naughty behavior is to be expected of toddlers from time to time, it wasn't customary or particularly tolerated in royal children.

In the months that followed, William's antics drew lots of attention from the media—and from the queen. Elizabeth strongly disapproved of the lack of discipline provided by Diana, Barbara Barnes, and, in particular, her eldest son.

Although Charles could be a bit more strict than Diana and the nanny, and he had cut back considerably on his official obligations right after Harry was born, he nevertheless spent less time with William and Harry and had less influence over their behavior. On top of that, he was reluctant to repeat with his own sons the mistakes his sometimes harsh and always distant father had made with him.

Both Charles and Diana were determined that Harry, with his brother, William, were to be a new breed of royal. Whether they could pull off their bold new approach to parenting the princes remained to be seen.

IMPORTANT DATES IN HARRY'S LIFE

November 14, 1948: Prince Charles was born.

July 1, 1961: Diana Spencer was born.

February 6, 1981: Prince Charles and Lady Diana Spencer became engaged.

July 29, 1981: Prince Charles and Lady Diana Spencer were married.

June 21, 1982: Prince William was born at St. Mary's Hospital, Paddington, London.

September 15, 1984: Prince Harry was born at St. Mary's Hospital, Paddington, London.

December 21, 1984: Prince Harry was christened at St. George's Chapel, Windsor Castle.

December 9, 1992: Prince Charles and Princess Diana's separation was announced.

August 28, 1996: Prince Charles and Princess Diana were divorced.

August 30, 1997: Princess Diana was killed in a car accident in Paris, France.

March 19, 2000: Prince Harry was confirmed at the Eton College Chapel.

CHAPTER 3

The Early Years

The first year of Harry's life was spent mainly at Kensington and Highgrove, with his brother as a constant—and willing—playmate. The boys got along famously and affectionately, with Harry toddling along imitating his older sibling's antics, as kid brothers are prone to do.

They spent nearly all their time together, even sharing the night nursery at the palace, which was a cozy attic room despite the windows that were barred for security. At the foot of each of their little beds was a wooden chest filled with their favorite toys. Harry reportedly snuggled with a stuffed Snoopy every night.

By day, he spent most of his time next door in the day nursery with William and his nannies. The large, pleasant room was painted soft yellow and in chilly weather a fire crackled cozily in the fireplace. The furniture was from Dragons, a posh London store, and was hand-painted with colorful animals. The boys ate their meals together at a small wooden table, and Diana sometimes joined them, especially for afternoon tea.

The walls were lined with bookcases and cabinets for the boys' many toys and games. They had a fleet of small cars, puzzles, stuffed animals, and an army of toy soldiers. There was a rocking horse sent to them by American first lady Nancy Reagan, and Jumbo, a rolling stuffed elephant that had once belonged to their father.

Harry and William shared their own private bathroom adjacent to the nursery, and it had child-size sinks and toilets. The nannies' quarters were right down the hall, and Diana and Charles's rooms were one floor below.

In nice weather Harry loved romping in the palace gardens. The whole family enjoyed the rooftop garden in particular. Although it was located several stories up, in the heart of bustling London, it was much like an American backyard, equipped with lounges for sunbathing, a swing set, and a grill for family barbecues. The royals even grew their own tomatoes in a greenhouse there.

Harry learned to swim in his own private pools, and to ride on his own horse, a Shetland pony called Smokey. The animal was kept, along with William's pony, Trigger, at Highgrove, the family's weekend house in Gloucestershire.

Harry looked up to William as a role model, and they both looked up to their father. However, Charles wasn't home very often, for his travels had begun to take him around the world again. He seemed to be slacking off a bit in the parental duties he had once tackled so enthusiastically and so regularly. Harry's father once again seemed caught up in the many obligations that came with being Prince of Wales, along with his own interests like polo, fishing, and gardening.

On the other hand, Diana, whose bedroom wasn't far from the palace nursery, spent as much time as possible with her children. She comforted them when they had nightmares or were sick, on occasion climbing into their beds with them or bringing them into hers for cuddles and kisses.

She often joined them to splash in the palace pool, and she rode horses with them even though she wasn't crazy about riding. She had been injured in a childhood accident and wasn't much of an equestrienne, unlike the other royal women.

Diana took them to McDonald's for burgers and fries, and to see Santa at Selfridges, a London department store. On such outings, Diana always made it clear that she and her sons would wait in line with everyone else. She didn't want the princes treated differently from other children, as her husband's generation of royals had been.

In keeping with her mission to make Harry and William normal boys, Diana made a point to dress them casually in jeans and baseball caps whenever possible. She shopped for their clothes herself, and like thousands of other kids, they wore brands like Osh-Kosh B'Gosh and Benetton, even Mickey Mouse sweatshirts.

A compassionate woman who was always aware of those less fortunate than she, Diana knew that her sons wouldn't be aware of the suffering endured by many in the world unless she made it a point to expose them to the grim reality. She wanted them to understand their privileged positions, and to feel a sense of responsibility toward those who could benefit from their help. At this stage in her life, the young mother was beginning to find her footing in her own work with the poor and the sick. She wanted her sons to share her empathy—and perhaps someday, to carry on in her place.

Until Harry's generation, the royal children had been raised in gilded cages, with little interaction with or exposure to the world outside the palace gates. Thanks to their mother, Harry and William were able to relate to those less fortunate, endearing them to people who might otherwise have resented their position.

Although the royal family worked hard much of the time, they also played hard. Harry was surrounded by the trappings of wealth: fine vacation homes, yachts, private planes. He ventured far beyond the castle gates as a young boy, visiting foreign countries and meeting dignitaries from other lands. He often spent summer vacations in Majorca with the Spanish royal family. He learned the importance of fresh air and exercise and from an early age indulged in favorite royal pursuits like skiing, riding, shooting, and fishing.

Both Diana and Charles were somewhat permissive and doted on their sons—perhaps a bit too much. With an entire staff at their beck and call, and parents who were determined to cuddle them at every opportunity, the boys—William in particular—were becoming overindulged. The Prince and Princess of Wales had to do something about it before the future king get a reputation for being a spoiled brat.

Eventually—when Harry was two—Nanny Barbara Barnes would leave the household, after continued conflict about how the young princes were to be disciplined in her care. She was reportedly overindulgent with the children, who, with excessive attention heaped on them wherever they went, were in need of strict boundaries at home.

Barbara Barnes was replaced by Ruth Wallace,

a kindly, no-nonsense woman who had worked for other royals, including King Constantine of Greece and Princess Michael of Kent. Harry was just learning to speak when Ruth came along, and the best he could manage was to call her "Roof." As a result, she became forever known to the boys as "Nanny Roof." On her first public outing after being hired in March 1987, she wheeled a smiling Harry, well bundled against the chill, in Kensington Gardens.

Less liberal than Nanny Barnes had been, Ruth Wallace—assisted by Olga Powell, who remained with the family—disciplined the boys when necessary and taught them to respect the household staff.

The plan had been for William and Harry to be educated at home by a governess during their preschool years. That, after all, was royal tradition. However, Diana convinced Charles that their sons not only needed to learn how to behave properly, but they also needed to learn how to play with other children their own ages.

So, after a year at home together, the brothers were forced to go their separate ways. Just days after his first birthday, on September 24, 1985, little Harry bid three-year-old William farewell as his brother was sent off to nursery school at Mrs. Mynor's School in Notting Hill Gate, about ten minutes from the palace. William seemed unfazed by the milestone or the cameras that recorded the big moment.

The year that followed saw William receiving more and more bad press. A July 7, 1986, story in *People* magazine was headlined "William the Terrible" and listed some of the future king's more rambunctious stunts, such as pushing his way to the front of lines and bullying other kids on the playground to the point where they began to call him "Billy the Basher."

"William's very enthusiastic about things. He just pushes himself right into it," Diana said. "By comparison, Harry is quieter and just watches. Number two skates in quite nicely."

Next to his hell-raising older brother, small thumb-sucking Harry came across as particularly agreeable. *People* magazine reported that "while Wills receives public scoldings from his nannies, Harry get public cleanings after smearing chocolate, strawberries, or whatever else he's eating on his face."

The magazine went on to say, "The introverted Harry adores his older brother but resents reminders of Will's greater skills; William protects his little brother but likes to be in charge."

By the time William turned five, in June 1987, he showed signs of better behavior. When during one of their father's polo matches, he and two-year-old Harry climbed into an ambulance to play, onlookers concerned about Harry's well-being in his temperamental brother's company soon realized he was in good hands. He allowed his older brother to gently strap him to a stretcher and give him a thorough checkup.

In September 1987, two years after William started nursery school, Harry followed in his brother's footsteps. Unlike William, he was tentative about the prospect of leaving the shelter of home, and perhaps about the press coverage, too.

The day he started at Mrs. Mynor's—accompanied, of course, by his detective—he was nervous and reluctant to leave his familiar home behind. Yet when confronted by the barrage of reporters waiting to capture his big moment, his sense of mischief took hold and he made ridiculous faces at the cameras, much to his mother's amusement.

There was something adorable—and sweetly vulnerable—about the younger of the two princes bravely venturing out into the world that had cynically dubbed him "the Spare." Author Meredith Graham wrote a touching fictionalized story on the topic. It was called "The Scaredy Cats" and appeared in the February 1990 issue of *Ladies' Home Journal* magazine.

The piece, pure fiction, is written from little

Harry's viewpoint and takes place the night before he starts school for the first time. It captures his insecurities about leaving home, his frustrations about being the younger brother of the somewhat spoiled and rambunctious heir to the throne, and, most poignantly, Harry's close relationship and dependence on his beloved and beautiful "Mummy."

In the story, Diana comforts him in the dark night nursery, telling him about her own secret fears of facing a world full of strangers, and helps him cope with the changes ahead. At the end, of course, he summons his courage, lifts his little chin, and journeys off to school.

That's what happened in reality, too. It took Harry a while, but once he settled into the cheerful classroom, he learned to enjoy preschool's casual atmosphere. At first he was too shy to even speak to the teachers, but eventually he found his voice. It helped that there, as at home, he was called "Harry" instead of by his full title.

The three dozen enrolled students might have been from some of London's most privileged families, but the environment at Mrs. Mynor's was similar to nursery schools everywhere.

The children were surrounded by cheerful educational toys and books. They did arts and crafts, performed music, learned their letters and numbers. They had snack time, played outside on pleasant days, and learned to get along with others. There were three levels of learning in the school, based on age. Students started as Cygnets, moved up to Little Swans, and became Big Swans before graduating.

This was Harry's first chance to establish his own identity outside the walls of the palace. With his bright red hair and sweetly shy grin, he was an adorable child who charmed his teachers and fellow students in his own right. Yet inevitably, he found himself compared to William. On one occasion he threw a tantrum when his attempts at a clay sculpture were dismissed by an elder as inferior to his older brother's.

At nursery school, Harry had his share of chances to steal the spotlight. He performed in several school plays and played a shepherd in the school's nativity pageant in 1988. He had lots of friends and was frequently seen outside of Mrs. Mynor's in the company of other little schoolboys.

Once it was decided that Harry and William should mingle with other children, every effort was made to give them a "normal" lifestyle. While they were showered with gifts wherever they went, Diana decided that they could choose and keep only one item—although they eventually realized that Mummy could be persuaded to give in on occasion if they pestered her enough.

Harry loved to romp at London playgrounds and at Windsor Safari Park, the first of many amusement parks he would enjoy in his young life, thanks to his fun-loving mother. He was introduced to country life on the family's weekends at Highgrove, and came to relish the outdoorsy lifestyle his father craved and his mother abhorred. Spirited and energetic, Harry rode bicycles, cheered his father at his polo matches, and galloped around with dogs, as boys do around the world.

But Harry's days also regularly included royal duties that couldn't be avoided. As a tiny toddler, he learned to salute and shake hands. On Thursday afternoons, Harry went to tea with his grandmother, the queen, whom he called "Granny." The pint-size prince was frequently required to dress like a miniature gentleman in a suit and tie, and to sit still during speeches and ceremonies that seemed endless to a boy who dearly loved to frolic and play.

As the offspring of the most famous couple in the world, Harry was constantly on display. During the princes' early childhood years, William seemed to take the cameras in stride more than Harry, who seemed to cringe back from the limelight at times. He appeared distinctly uncomfortable in some early photographs and films.

Once, when he was about four, he defiantly stuck his tongue out at a throng of reporters, only to be harshly reprimanded by William, who caught him in the act. Still, Harry often appeared in his brother's protective shadow when they were in public. At times, William seemed to be shielding little Harry from the glare of the cameras.

Of course, the boys were only human, and they didn't always get along perfectly. There were naturally brotherly scuffles and scrapes. William, who reportedly bullied, teased, and hit other children at nursery school, once even dangled small Harry by his ankles from a window at Windsor Castle.

According to some reports, William was known to brag to other children about the fact that one day he would be king. Anyone can imagine it would have been hard for him to resist doing the same to his little brother during the course of normal sibling arguments. Harry, for his part, once said that if William decided he didn't want to take over the throne, he would be more than happy to step in. "I shall be King Harry," he declared cheerfully—and maybe even a bit wistfully.

There's no doubt that there are times when, like any younger sibling, Harry must resent the fact that William—in addition to being heir to the British throne—gets to cross each milestone years before Harry has a chance to catch up.

Even their parents admitted that the boys fought with each other from time to time. Once their mother supposedly referred to her sons affectionately as "a couple of little thugs," and their father pointed out that when they got upset with each other, you had to watch out for "flying tractors."

Dr. Dorothy Einon, a child psychologist at the University College in London, was quoted as saying, "It may well be that Harry will be allowed to get away with things simply because he isn't being groomed for the role that William is . . . it's very common for brothers and sisters to fight. Older children always bully younger ones."

But as much as Harry might get on William's nerves in the way kid brothers can, William was the first to come to his defense if anyone dared hurt Harry in any way. Theirs was a normal brotherly relationship.

Overall, Harry was a contented child whose days were as routine as possible within the extraordinary circumstances of the royal household. While his nanny always got him out of bed in the morning and prepared him for the day ahead, Harry was able to count on seeing his parents, if they were around, before they headed off to work. If at all possible, Diana even drove him to school herself—accompanied by their ever-present security detail, of course—and she tried to give him his evening bath, read him his bedtime story, and tuck him into bed at night.

Still, Harry must have missed his beloved Mummy when she couldn't be with him, and he certainly must have been aware that his home life was far different from the lives of other children he met.

He must also have realized that his parents were miserable together. By 1987 they were leading separate lives, something that was increasingly apparent to the press, although the couple remained married well into the next decade. Charles was, at this point, heavily involved with his married mistress, Camilla Parker Bowles, once again. Diana, who had once despaired over her husband's extramarital relationship, now seemed indifferent to it. She would later admit to infidelities of her own.

As Harry grew older, it became rare for the family to appear together in public. Frequently

Diana and the boys were captured as a three-some, with Charles apparently having faded into the background as his marriage disintegrated.

Yet on holidays such as Christmas, the press would be invited to photograph the extended royal family, and every effort would be made to convince the world that everything was perfectly normal, that everyone was perfectly blissful.

When Harry was three, he was rushed to the hospital for an emergency hernia operation. Diana kept a round-the-clock vigil at his bedside. Charles, who was in Turkey at the time—reportedly on vacation with Camilla Parker Bowles—didn't return home. He would later, according to biographer Anthony Holden's *Charles at Fifty*, say that he had offered to return, only to be told by Diana that it wasn't necessary.

No matter. By then, the press had formed its opinions of the Wales royals as parents, and had overwhelmingly sided with Diana, depicting Charles as a cold, uncaring father. Photos and films of an affectionate Charles with his boys in later years would seem to ultimately dispute that image. Yet the simple truth remains: Harry didn't see much of his father as a young boy.

He grew very attached to his bodyguard,

Sergeant David Sharp. Unlike Harry's father, the good-natured man was with the child around the clock, and was willing to play with Harry and William, even getting down into the sand and building castles on a beach during an August 1988 royal visit to Majorca.

That September, Harry celebrated his fourth birthday, but the party his parents threw for him was ruined when he learned that his buddy David Sharp wouldn't be there. Charles, concerned about how attached Harry had become to the man, had absolutely forbidden him from attending. Poor Harry was in tears. Not long after that, Diana had Sharp switched over to her staff as her bodyguard, which meant he was still in the boys' lives, but wouldn't bond as closely with them.

While this might seem coldhearted, the truth is that it's dangerous for security detail to become emotionally involved with the people they're supposed to watch over. Those who guard children are particularly prone to such behavior, as it can be difficult to maintain professional detachment from a vulnerable child—particularly, a little boy who desperately longs for a male role model.

Still, for all the troubles—not to mention pomp and circumstance—of his formative years, Harry managed to emerge as a remarkably well-adjusted boy. By 1989, when he completed the Big Swans form at nursery school, he was eager to move on to the next adventure: Kensington's renowned Wetherby School.

CHAPTER 4

Off to School

A day school for boys aged four to eight, exclusive Wetherby drew the sons of London's finest families. Here, in addition to his regular studies, Harry would learn the polished, gentlemanly behavior that was expected of a young prince.

William had attended Wetherby for two years by the time Harry's turn came along. Again, Harry's big brother had paved the way for him; the school's teachers and fellow students were by now accustomed to having royalty in their midst.

It was perhaps at this point in Harry's life that he became acutely aware of the constant comparison to his older brother. Yet the younger Windsor more than measured up, making a strong impression on those around him, and he somewhat surprisingly outshone his brother academically. He was considered highly intelligent and was placed with the brightest group of students at the school.

One of his teachers was quoted at the time, in *Ladies' home Journal* magazine, as saying, "Harry was a bit shy to begin with, but now that he's settled in, he loves it. He plays so well with the other children."

He was eased into the academic world, with his first year's studies including "fun" classes such as storytelling and model-making. Harry's natural athletic ability was also encouraged at Wetherby, a school that stimulated students' sporting involvement with annual traditions such as the school gala held every March at Jubilee Sports Center in west London, and the Annual Sports Day held at Richmond Athletic Ground.

The latter was a family event, and Harry's parents always joined in the fray, participating in relays and sack races along with the crowd, much to their son's delight.

Harry's weekdays were in some ways typical of any American youngster's. He woke early and ate breakfast before going to school. He was required to wear a uniform, which consisted of a scarlet-trimmed gray jacket and cap with the school crest on the pocket, white shirt and red necktie, gray socks, dress shoes, and dark-colored shorts—even in the chill of winter!

Harry's daily lessons included the traditional

reading, math, and geography, as well as comput-
ers, foreign languages, sports, and a strong em-
phasis on music. Wetherby students were able to
show off their exceptional musical and thespian
skills at annual plays and Christmas concerts attended by their parents and friends.

During one of those holiday concerts, six-year-
old Harry sang a solo as his mother watched from
the audience, beaming with pride, then applaud-
ing wildly.

After each school day was over, Harry would
be driven home to the palace. On lucky afternoons, his beloved mother was waiting to greet
him with a hug and kiss, ready to hear all about
his day.

It is the British custom to have daily tea in the
late afternoon. A meal in itself, tea falls between
lunch and dinner (which is usually served later in
the evening in England than it is in American
families). At tea, Harry—who reportedly had a
healthy appetite for junk food, like most children—would eat traditional cakes, muffins, or
sandwiches.

Dinner was a more formal affair, but Harry—
unlike many children his age—didn't dine
nightly with both his parents, only with his
brother, aside from rare occasions when one or
both of their parents joined them.

There are a few reasons for this.

One is that the demanding schedules of Charles and Diana were crammed with speeches, appearances, charity events, and other obligations that took them away from home during the evenings.

Another is that by the time Harry was enrolled at Wetherby, Charles had all but moved out of Kensington Palace. He was living at Highgrove, the family's country estate. On Friday afternoons, Harry and William—and occasionally Diana—would be driven the hundred miles west of London to join him there.

Charles's parenting skills were now the subject of intense scrutiny in the press. The media took note in May 1991 when Harry spent his school break alone with Diana, who brought him to visit a Royal Air Force base and a wild-animal park. Charles was nowhere to be seen.

And when, less than two weeks later, William was injured at school, Diana dropped everything and rushed to the hospital thirty-six miles away. Prince Charles did the same thing. William's skull had been fractured and he underwent a seventy-minute surgery to repair the damage.

Afterward, a worried Diana kept a round-the-clock vigil at his bedside. A concerned Harry was allowed to skip school in order to visit William as soon as he was allowed to after the surgery.

Charles, meanwhile, kept his royal engagement: a performance of *Tosca* at the Royal Opera House.

"WHAT KIND OF DAD ARE YOU?" screamed a headline in the *Sun*.

The answer was simple: the royal kind. Charles had never witnessed a warm father-son relationship firsthand. It was going to take a lot of practice, many years—and, sadly, a heartbreaking tragedy—for him to breach the gap with his sons, much less win parenting approval from the media.

As he grew older, Harry was allowed to join the older royals in their traditional weekend pursuits—hunting, shooting, fishing, and gardening. His father was in his element at Highgrove, while his mother found country life boring compared to London, where she enjoyed the shops, restaurants, and theater.

Diana was particularly miserable in the summers, when the family would travel to its Scottish retreat at Balmoral. Consisting of a granite mansion on the banks of the Dee River in the shadow of the famed Lochnagar, the estate had been in the family since Harry's great-great-great-grandmother Victoria and her husband, Albert (for whom Harry was named), fell in love with its rustic charm in the mid-nineteenth century.

In this remote Scottish countryside, the hectic royal schedule has always given way for ten weeks to a more casual atmosphere—so casual that even the queen dresses down in trousers and boots suitable for splashing through the muddy fields.

Days are mainly spent riding, fishing the streams, or hunting deer, rabbits, ducks, and pheasants. While the family often picnics outdoors during the afternoon and is even known to barbecue, dinner at Balmoral is always ceremonious, served from silver platters by red-uniformed servants.

At their family's highland hideaway, William and Harry learned early to embrace the Scottish heritage. They wore kilts and learned intricate dance steps such as the Highland Fling.

They romped with their cousins, Peter and Zara Phillips, Princess Anne's children, who were six and three years older than Harry, respectively, and Princesses Beatrice and Eugenie, Prince Andrew and Sara Ferguson's daughters, who were four and six years younger.

The royal grandchildren enjoyed their summer vacations at the family retreat, where in addition to traditional British sporting pursuits, they swam, hiked, and even went to the movies at the local cinema.

As he grew older, Harry did his best to behave properly in public, coached by his parents and even by his elder brother. But the fun-loving little boy couldn't always keep his lively spirits in check.

On one memorable occasion in 1990, the royal family had appeared in public at a ceremony to commemorate the Battle of Britain. During the solemn affair, six-year-old Harry grabbed the hands of his two-year-old cousin, Beatrice, and began dancing a jig with her—in full view of the public and, of course, the ever-present cameras. Harry's impulsive high jinks were captured for posterity, as was his mother's gentle admonishment.

On a later occasion, at a VJ day commemoration in 1995, Harry's boyish antics would again be memorably captured on video. As he stood dressed in a suit and tie, flanked by his brother and his by-then estranged parents at the official ceremony, he was visibly bored.

At first he merely fidgeted and checked his watch, but eventually, he could be seen bopping his head about, his mouth moving jauntily in time to the dignified music of the official marching band.

These rare glimpses of Harry's impish, adorable nature allow insight into the personality of a boy who is less reserved than his more regal older brother. Harry wasn't necessarily known as a troublemaker, as his brother had been as a toddler, but he did get into his share of boyish scrapes, such as being caught sneaking cigarettes at school.

Once, when he and William were playing at their uncle's estate, they accidentally locked themselves in a dungeon, and Scotland Yard had to be called to get them out.

A bit headstrong at times, Harry is apt to speak his mind, a trait that landed him in hot water with his parents from time to time.

According to several accounts, he once politely asked somebody for something other than what he'd been given, only to be reprimanded by Diana, who wanted to teach the boys their place—a place, that is, other than the one guaranteed by their royal birthright.

She expected them to wait in line when they went out in public, and despite a full staff of servants, to clean up after themselves—to an extent—at home.

Harry, by some accounts, rebelled at times— just as any red-blooded child is apt to do when confronted with parental authority.

On one memorable occasion, detailed in Christopher Andersen's *The Day Diana Died*, Diana said, "Oh, Harry, pick up your laundry."

The prince's cocky response, "Don't say, 'Oh, Harry.' "

Later, when the laundry still hadn't been removed, Diana snapped, "Oh, Harry, I told you to pick it up."

Harry is quoted in the book as saying, "It seems to me I asked you not to say, 'Oh, Harry.'" He then grabbed the laundry and fled his angry mother, in an age-old familiar domestic scene that has been, and will continue to be, repeated time and again in ordinary households around the world.

While they certainly clashed at times, as any mother and son will do, there appears to have been great affection between Diana and her younger son, and the sense that she protected him somewhat, aware that he was destined to grow up in William's shadow. They seemed to have had a warm, playful relationship, frequently evidenced in snapshots and film footage of the princess frolicking with athletic, adventurous Harry.

Once, after making a splash on a log flume ride at an amusement park, Harry promptly turned to his mother and audibly begged in his adorable English accent, "Mummy, can we do it again?"

Charles, too, appreciated Harry's sporting spirit. While the prince reportedly assumes that left-handed William will be unable to achieve much success playing polo, he feels that Harry shows great promise and natural ability as an athlete.

He has always nurtured Harry's interest in sports, providing him with soccer and badminton equipment, bicycles and motorbikes, even a trampoline was installed at Balmoral one memorable Easter.

When Harry visited Althorp, the Spencer family home, he was known to toboggan down the stairs on tea trays—with the permission of their uncle, the Earl Spencer. And *People* magazine said Harry was "bold on the ski slopes and a terror on the go-cart track."

Yet the magazine also noted that "he loves plants and animals and worships his older brother."

In September 1992, Harry's day-school days were behind him, when he joined William at Ludgrove School in Berkshire.

Secluded in a woodsy setting about twenty-five miles outside of London, the school's location allowed Harry a break from the constant press coverage of his life.

There, although he was away from home for the first time, he had little time to be lonely. Not only did he share a dorm room with several other boys, and a bathroom with many, but he was kept busy from morning until night, not just with his studies but also with extracurricular activities like swimming, tennis, soccer, and golf at the school's exclusive facilities.

The rules at Ludgrove would probably seem incredibly strict and old-fashioned to an American public-school student—the boys there weren't allowed to call home, they had to wear a navy blue uniform, and they had to be in bed with the lights out at eight o'clock.

Television shows were strictly limited, and newspapers were screened. Even listening to a Walkman when you were supposed to be asleep would land you in deep trouble with the headmaster.

The students were allowed eight weekends at home. On those occasions, Harry either went to see his mother in London or to his father's estate at Highgrove.

Undoubtedly, both Charles and Diana wanted what was best for their children, and tried hard to mend—and then mask—their troubled marriage as the years wore on.

Sadly, the charade couldn't last forever.

Before 1992 drew to a close, young Harry had to face the harsh reality that the parents who loved him dearly no longer—or perhaps never had—loved each other.

The Windsor Cousins

Sadly, all of Queen Elizabeth's grandchildren come from broken homes. Throughout his childhood, Harry has spent a significant amount of time with his four cousins, the offspring of his father's sister and brother, Princess Anne and Prince Andrew. The six royal grandchildren see each other on holidays, at official engagements, and, of course, each summer at Balmoral Castle.

Peter Phillips

Born Peter Mark Andrew Phillips on November 15, 1977, Peter is the son of Princess Anne and her ex-husband, Mark Phillips. Like Harry, he's athletic, handsome, and naturally charming, a positive role model who has taken Harry and William under his wing, treating them like younger brothers. Peter, and avid and skilled rugby player, attended Gordonstoun, the Scottish boarding school that had made Prince Charles so miserable, and is now enrolled at Exeter University, where he reportedly intends to major in sports medicine. When Harry was younger, it was Peter who spent lots of time teaching him to perfect his riding skills.

Zara Phillips

Peter's younger sister, Zara Anne Elizabeth Phillips, was born on May 15, 1981. The tall, pretty blonde has a bubble, upbeat, outgoing personality like her cousin Harry. She is also known as something of a royal rebel, having pierced her tongue and been caught in a boys' dorm room while away at boarding school—something that was strictly forbidden.

Princess Beatrice

Her Royal Highness Princess Beatrice Elizabeth Mary of York was born on August 8, 1988, to Prince Andrew and Sarah Ferguson, better known as "Fergie." With her strawberry blond hair and winning smile, she resembles her famous flame-haired mother. She enjoys sports, such as tennis, riding, and golf, and reportedly loves the color pink. Her mother, in her autobiography, calls her older daughter "musical and full of grace. She wears her heart on her sleeve."

Princess Eugenie

The youngest of the new royal generation, born March 23, 1990, has quite a name—Her

Royal Highness Princess Eugenie Victoria Helena of York. The perky redhead, who wasn't even two when her parents split, lives with her big sister, Andrew, and Fergie—who, in a unique arrangement, share a home and remain friends—at Sunninghill Park, near Windsor Castle. She and Beatrice regularly have tea with "Granny"—that's Queen Elizabeth to the rest of the world. Fergie, in her autobiography, says that Eugenie is "clever academically and appears lighthearted and easy. But she can surprise with her intensity, and she is fearlessly candid."

A Typical Virgo?

Harry's September 15 birthday places him in the six sign of the zodiac, Virgo. Third in line for the British throne, he would make a fine ruler, astrologically speaking. Virgos have an innate sense of duty, service, and working for the greater good.

Harry's easygoing nature and quick sense of humor are typical of those born under his zodiac sign, and so is his athletic energy. In fact, many Virgos are health nuts, devoted to vigorous workouts and good, clean living.

Often perfectionists, Virgos carry their high standards over to romance, and are devoted to making their relationships work. They can be detail-oriented, and are likely to pull out all stops when it comes to wooing a potential lover. While flirtatious, Harry is a long way from settling down. When the time comes to marry his ideal woman, she's quite likely to be a Capricorn, Pisces, or Aries, all signs that are exceptionally compatible with his.

CHAPTER 5

Divorce

The queen would later publicly—and with shocking candor—say that 1992 was an *"annus horribilis"* (horrible year) for the royal family.

The younger royals constantly made tabloid headlines. Harry's parents most frequently dominated the gossip, as the press endlessly speculated about the state of their marriage. Meanwhile, Harry's married aunt, Sara Ferguson, was photographed topless with another man. His grandfather, the Earl Spence, died suddenly of a heart attack in March.

In June a tell-all book called *Diana: Her True Story* was written by Andrew Morton, who later claimed—and was eventually backed by the princess—that Diana herself had cooperated with the project. The shocking biography revealed everything from her bulimia and suicide attempts to the details of her troubled married and Charles's infidelities.

On top of all this, a devastating fire nearly destroyed Windsor Castle in November, and there was a yearlong public clamor over the incredibly wealthy queen's exemption from paying income taxes.

But none of these calamities held a candle to the year's most shocking marital scandals. Before 1992 drew to a close, all three of the queen's married children found themselves single again. First, in March, came the announcement that Harry's uncle and godfather, Prince Andrew, was separating from Sarah Ferguson. Next, in April, Harry's aunt, Princess Anne, divorced Captain Mark Phillips. At three-thirty P.M. on December 9 came the year's most shocking—and to Harry, the most tragic—announcement. It was made by Prime Minister John Major to the House of Commons:

"It is announced from Buckingham Palace that with regret, the Prince and Princess of Wales have decided to separate. Their Royal Highnesses have no plans to divorce and their constitutional positions are unaffected. This decision has been reached amicably, and they will both continue to participate fully in the upbringing of their children.

The Queen and Duke of Edinburgh, though saddened, understand and sympathize with the difficulties which have led to this decision. They believe that a degree of privacy and understanding is essential if their Royal Highnesses are to provide a happy and secure upbringing for their children."

The news was no surprise to Harry, who was secluded at Ludgrove when it came. Diana had visited the school a few days earlier to tell Harry and his brother about it privately in the headmaster's office. Even then, it was probably expected to some extent.

Harry, who alone had remained living at home with his mother until three months before his parents officially split, knew the marriage was troubled, as much as Charles and Diana tried to keep it from him and William. Harry's departure for school that September before the separation, leaving Diana alone in the empty nest, may have helped to trigger the princess into taking action at last.

The family's Christmas card that fateful year—which had, until now, always pictured the four of them together—showed only William and Harry in a posed, formal shot. It would become a poignant symbol of that difficult holiday season.

However inevitable the news that his parents were splitting, Harry must have been devastated, although nobody knows precisely what happened when he gathered with his mother and brother in the headmaster's office that cold December day. Typically, in a household experiencing marital discord, the children hold out hope that somehow their parents will work things out in the end. Harry's hope had just been shattered.

Ludgrove's headmaster and other staff members attempted to shield Harry and William from the onslaught of press coverage, having already banned tabloid newspapers from the school in an effort to protect them. The announcement was purposely timed to coincide with the boys' holiday break to allow them an ample period of time to digest the news away from the pressures of school. Harry's last few days of the term after the announcement were spent in the usual Christmas plays and choral concerts, but the merriment around him must have rung hollow in the little boy's heart that season.

After seeing his mother at Kensington Palace, Harry spent that Christmas at the Sandringham estate, as he had spent every other Christmas of his eight years.

But his mother—for the first time—wasn't with him for the holiday—and he had no choice about the matter. Even if he had wanted to spend Christmas with his mother and the Spencer relatives at Althorp, his grandmother's wishes took priority. The queen wanted William and Harry to carry on the royal tradition of Christmas at Sandringham, regardless of the state of their parents' marriage.

On the heels of the palace's announcement that both Harry's parents would cooperate in raising him and William, the holiday situation sent a clear message to the public: The boys belonged with their father, the heir to the throne, and not with their mother. According to *U.S. News and World Report*, this was at a time when nine out of every ten English mothers got custody rights in a divorce.

There is no question that this was a difficult Christmas for Harry. He and William weren't the only Windsor children spending their first Christmas apart from their mother. Little Beatrice and Eugenie, too, were forced to spend the holiday with their father and the queen while their mother, Sarah Ferguson, was left, uninvited, only two miles away at a cottage on the estate. Meanwhile, at least one member of the family was in a celebratory mood: Princess Anne was newly remarried, having wed Captain Tim Laurence in a secret ceremony only a few days earlier.

Prince Charles clearly tried to comfort Harry and William in the wake of the separation announcement that December. He was frequently photographed out walking and hunting with the boys during those days at Sandringham. And the rest of the royals undoubtedly did their best to cheer Harry and William. The boys' grandparents, formal as they are, truly care about their well-being.

Yet even surrounded by a family that loved him, Harry discovered that his Christmas at Sandringham wasn't exactly a relaxing vacation, even in the best of times. Life there is anything but casual, and it isn't as though a boy is allowed to wallow around in sweatpants, drowning his sorrows in television and junk food. There are official photo calls, visits by dignitaries, a schedule to be followed. The family Christmas dinner is a black-tie affair, and their walk to church services on Christmas Day is watched by thousands of onlookers and filmed to appear on television around the world.

After six days apart from Mummy, Harry flew with her and William to Nevis, a Caribbean Island, for a vacation. But even then, he was uncomfortably aware that things had changed forever. For one thing, they took a commercial airline flight. For another, he and William sat up in first class while their mother rode in economy.

Once they landed, to everyone's relief, things got back to normal—at least, to some extent. Harry and William frolicked on the sunny, palm-tree-dotted beaches and in the sparkling blue-green water, unaware—perhaps at first—that a new scandal was brewing back in England.

On January 12, 1993, the press published transcripts of a telephone call between Prince Charles and his mistress, Camilla Parker Bowles. The conversation, taped without their knowledge a few years earlier, was filled with sexual innuendo and left no doubt that they were involved in a long-time secret romance.

Likewise, tapes of a call between Princess Diana and her friend James Gibley had been published. Though their conversation was less sexually explicit, they also hinted at a romantic relationship. Even worse, Diana bad-mouthed the royal family, including Charles.

Any child would be embarrassed and humiliated to have a parent's infidelities or marital discords publicly revealed. In these extraordinary circumstances, the details of Harry's parents' extramarital relationships—and their disdain for each other—were splashed in newspapers around the world. All this, coming on the heels of the official separation announcement, must have made it incredibly difficult for Harry to return to school for a new term early in 1993, where he had to face his classmates, all of whom undoubtedly knew what was going on.

Although the Ludgrove officials did their best to keep the gossip and teasing in check, anyone who has ever been a schoolchild knows how brutal children can be. There is no doubt that Harry had some fast growing up to do in those early months of 1993. Only eight, he was facing and coming to terms with one ugly reality after another.

Ingrid Seward, editor of *Majesty* magazine and author of *Royal Children*, observed that William had become introverted in the wake of his parents' divorce. William, she noted, "would feel that somehow it was his fault, whereas Harry is a happy-go-lucky little chap and bounces along."

Or so it seemed.

Harry did his best to ignore the ugly rumblings and hold his head high when seen in public, looking for all the world like he had emerged unscathed from the breakdown of his family. He was even pictured smiling in one memorable front-page photo—perched cozily upon the lap of the reason for his newfound happiness.

Alexandra—better known as "Tiggy"—Legge-Bourke entered Harry's life at a time when he was dealing with a turmoil he must have then, naively, thought would be the worst thing he'd ever have to face. Little did he know that before he even made it to his teens, darker days would descend. Then, as now, he would seek comfort in the arms of the pretty, fun-loving nanny with the silly-sounding nickname.

Tiggy's aristocratic family had long been acquainted with the royal family. After his separation from Diana, Charles hired the outgoing thirty-year-old as a nanny who would help look after his sons whenever they were with him.

Easygoing Harry took to Tiggy right away. She was athletic and outdoorsy, and accompanied him on his favorite pursuits, such as riding, fishing, hunting, and hiking. She was like an older sister who teased him and allowed him to tease her in return. Together they romped the fields of Charles's Highgrove estate and the grounds of Balmoral, with Tiggy in a role Harry's mother had never willingly occupied. Harry's nanny, unlike his mother, was more than game to join in the traditional outdoorsy royal activities, and her breezy, sporting attitude was exactly what he needed during those trying times.

Still, he must have been torn, out of loyalty to his mother. Diana, like any mother would be, was jealous of Tiggy' presence in her sons' lives. She had been banished from a part of their lives that Tiggy was able to share.

Yet she must have been grateful on some level to see photos of them smiling and contented—

even when they weren't with her. However bitter her relationship with Charles, she couldn't have wanted their sons to suffer miserably on occasions when they were in his care.

Besides, she, too, continued to employ a nanny. Olga Powell was still working at Kensington Palace, keeping an eye on the boys when their mother could not.

It is said Diana, who was interested in alternative medicine, was particularly concerned about the usual outgoing Harry's tendency to lock his feelings inside after the divorce. She reportedly took him to a practitioner who put a skin patch on him so that he would be able to release his emotions and continue to heal.

In most divorce situations, children are forced to adapt to spending much less time with one parent—usually the father. However, Harry's situation proved to be the opposite. The legal separation agreement allowed for Harry and William to spend equal time with their parents. This meant that the boys saw more of their father now than they ever had before.

So, in a sense, there was a silver lining: The end of the marriage meant the beginning of a father-son bond that would become especially crucial in later years. For the first time, Harry spent "quality" time with his father on a regular basis, and Charles, to his credit, seems to have done his absolute best to ease his sons' transition through that difficult period in their lives.

They were even photographed that spring proudly helping him prepare for a polo match at Windsor Great Park, with Harry on the ground lacing his father's boots for him.

Yet there is no question that, even with his parents' devotion and Tiggy's upbeat presence, Harry's closest ally at this time in his life was his brother, William.

The two boys had adored each other from Harry's first full day on earth, when his brother showed up to cuddle and coo over him at the hospital. Now they were in a unique situation.

Nobody else in the world could possibly know what it was like to be the offspring of the century's most celebrated, and perhaps most publicly tormented, couple. Only Harry and William shared the burden of their legacy, and although not everything in the brothers' lives is destined to be fairly divided, they equally shouldered the pain and the challenges as their family shattered around them.

It has been said that William was more protective than ever of his kid brother during their years together at Ludgrove—especially when their schoolmates decided to give one or both of them a hard time about being royal. If Harry ever found himself in more trouble than he could handle, he turned to William, who could always be counted on to intervene on Harry's behalf.

So, William and Harry leaned on each other through the worst of times—again, foreshadowing the far more terrible trials that lay ahead.

But as 1993 progressed, the unsuspecting Harry must have thought the worst was behind him. Now that everything was out in the open, life settled into a routine punctuated by frequent holidays with one or the other of his parents. His father took him to Italy and the Greek Islands.

His mother took him skiing in Austria in March, but while the royal threesome was in the picturesque town of Lech, they were harassed by photographers to the point where it turned ugly and the police had to intervene. Both William and Harry were shaken by this, as was their mother. But the boys were by now learning to shrug off such incidents as a part of their lives that would never change.

And despite the hassles caused by the media, Diana persisted in giving her sons at least the illusion of a "normal" life. During the Easter holiday, she brought Harry and William to watch motor racing at Donnington Park. Instead of arriving in a chauffeured limousine, the boys showed up in a plain old Ford station wagon with their mom at the wheel. For a few precious moments, they could actually forget who and what they were, enjoying something that suburban kids everywhere take for granted.

In the summer, without the regular routine of school as a distraction, Harry confronted the reality of their parents' separation by spending long periods of time with each of them—and without them. Once—while Charles was playing polo, and Diana was in Zimbabwe—daredevil Harry was thrilled to have Formula-1 driver Jackie Stewart escort him around the Silverstone track.

Yet, despite perks like that, his life that summer wasn't much different on the surface from most kids'. He and William and lunch with Diana at London's Planet Hollywood in June and rode their bikes together, dressed in jeans and T-shirts, at Kensington Gardens in July.

Yet Harry could never quite forget that he wasn't like other kids. The summer of 1993 marked an important milestone for him. In July he made his official debut as a "working royal," when he traveled to Germany with Diana. There, they visited the Light Dragoons regiment, something that Harry, who had at the time a passion for all things military, fully relished.

On August 2, back in London, Diana took him and William to a screening of *Jurassic Park* in Leicester Square. When a photographer snapped their picture afterward, a frazzled Diana screamed, "You make my life hell!"

She was clearly becoming fed up with the constant paparazzi coverage, and reeling from the ongoing stress of the separation. Still, she hadn't forgotten how to unwind and relax. On August 4, the royal family gathered at Clarence House to celebrate the ninety-third birthday of Harry's great-grandmother, the Queen Mother. But Harry wasn't at the party; he was with his mother, whooping it up at a go-cart course at Buckmore Park in Kent.

The boys rejoined their father's side of the family when they went to Scotland in mid-August with Charles. They traveled by train, and an account of the trip in the *Sun* reported that, "the young princes looked awkward and uncomfortable in stiff, old-fashioned (clothes). Glum William and Harry . . . walked three paces behind their dad in total silence. They were a far cry from the boisterous boys who giggle happily when they are out with Princess Di."

At Balmoral, William and Harry fell quickly into a happy routine, rising early every morning in true country style and sitting down at precisely 7:45 A.M. to have a hot breakfast with their father. They did their usual hunting, hiking, and fishing; although this year, they were filmed doing this for an ITV documentary Charles had agreed to. The footage of the three Windsor men on the banks of Lock Muick suggests that they were engaging in some old-fashioned male bonding, and the boys both seemed to be having a fabulous time with their dad.

Not to be outdone, Diana flew Harry, his brother, and some of their friends via British Airways to Orlando, Florida, on August 24. There, they checked into Disney World's posh Grand Floridian Hotel, where they stayed in the marble-floored Presidential Suite, complete with a pool view and private elevator.

Naturally, the press went wild. Harry was captured on film shrieking delightedly on Splash Mountain and enjoying Big Thunder Mountain Railroad, the Jungle Cruise, and other attractions. They visited the Indiana Jones Epic Stunt Spectacular at Disney-MGM Studios Theme Park.

For security purposes, Diana agreed that for once the boys wouldn't have to wait in line like everyone else. They were escorted directly onto each ride, and they got around the park through a network of underground tunnels reserved for staff and VIPs. Naturally Harry's bodyguards were directly behind him at all times, even on rides. Still, the security, the press, and the gawking tourists don't seem to have put much of a damper on the trip.

Both Charles and Diana continued to appear frequently in the press, but more often now it was in connection with their various good works rather than scandals. Both the prince and princess were advocates for many charities, but it was Diana who generally got the most press coverage, often photographed and filmed touring hospitals, orphanages, and homeless shelters.

In November, though, Harry's world was rocked again when the *Sunday Mirror* published front-page photos of his mother, an unwitting subject. A hidden camera planted at her private gym had captured the scantily clad princess working out.

Outraged, Diana sued the newspaper and the photographer. A settlement agreement spared her—and the royal family—a trial, but the damage was done. Once again, the press was in an uproar. Diana felt hounded and overwhelmed.

On December 3, 1993, nearly a year after the prime minister's announcement of her separation from Charles, Diana made an equally startling public proclamation when she tearfully said that she would essentially be withdrawing from public life in part to be with her sons, "who deserve as much love, care, and attention as I am able to give."

By all accounts, she lived up to her promise during the next three and a half years of Harry's life—years that would turn out to be the last of her own.

The Child of a Broken Home

Harry isn't the first little boy whose parents went their separate ways, and he won't be the last. Although his wealth and royal blood have privileged him in many ways, nothing protected him from the problems that come with divorce. Nobody, not even a prince, emerges unscathed from such a traumatic ordeal.

In his book *Growing Up With Divorce*, Neil Kalter, PhD, notes that children who are early elementary age when their parents separate, as Harry was, are prone to a number of emotional reactions. The most common is an overwhelming sense of sadness. Others are depression, anger, and anxiety.

After all, the biggest issue children face during a divorce is the change in family lifestyle as they have always know it. When parents separate, a father (or, less commonly, a mother) typically moves out of the family home, leaving the child to spend most of his time with a single parent. Often financial issues compound the stress.

In Harry's case, his parents were already

living separate lives. His father had gradually moved out of Kensington Palace years earlier. Partly because of this, and partly due to the prince's and princess's busy schedules, the young prince was already used to spending time with his parents individually.

Also, he was living away at boarding school when the separation was announced. And certainly, because of his family's wealth, there were no money problems to affect him directly. So ultimately, although his life had irrevocably changed, his day-to-day circumstances, for the most part, weren't altered.

Ultimately, though, his parents' divorce was very painful for Harry. His daily routine wasn't significantly altered, but he had to deal with something that other kids don't: the whole world watching and analyzing his and his family's every move. Living in a royal fishbowl means he couldn't possibly have had time or space to absorb the changes privately.

Former *Newsweek* editor Linda Bird Francke, in her book *Growing Up Divorced*, says that a child who is between the ages of six and eight when his parents split, as Harry was, will "go through a period of intense pain."

Citing a study of children this age conducted by Joan Kelly and Judith Wallerstein, Francke notes that "not one of them was happy with the divorce, even where there had been histories of chronic and even violent conflict. More than anything else, these children want their parents back together."

Undoubtedly, Harry secretly hoped that his mother and father would reconcile their differences. Sadly, that never happened, although in the year leading up to Diana's death, they appeared to have reached a point where, for the sake of Harry and William, they could tolerate—perhaps even appreciate—each other.

As a child of divorce, it is likely that Harry won't enter into marriage lightly when his turn comes. Hopefully, unlike his father before him, he will be allowed to wed out of love and not duty, making a mutually supportive, loving lifelong match.

CHAPTER 6

Growing Up

As Harry approached his tenth birthday, he was a jolly, free-spirited boy who seemed to be enjoying life to its fullest. His uncle, the Earl Spencer, once called him a "mischievous imp," and his mother said, in light of his fondness for pulling pranks, "Harry's the naughty one—just like me."

He was becoming a fine rider and a skilled skier, showing more natural aptitude for both these sports than his older brother ever had.

Yet William was now outshining him academically at Ludgrove. While Harry had begun his educational career as an advanced student, he was finding it more difficult to achieve the high grades that others might have expected of him. It couldn't have helped that his family continued to rule the tabloid press, a continuing source of stress for the young prince.

Until now, Prince Charles had largely been seen as the villain as his royal marriage unraveled. But in 1994, the tables turned to some extent as the ongoing media coverage turned against Diana. Now she, too, was being blamed for the breakup of the marriage.

Two specific events seem to have triggered this change. The first, in August, was the published report that Diana had been accused of making obsessive phone calls to Oliver Hoare, a married-with-children millionaire art dealer to whom she had recently been linked. Harry knew Hoare, who often visited his mother at the palace, but he probably had no idea that Diana was romantically involved with him, until it was trumpeted in the papers.

The second pivotal event of 1994 was perhaps more devastating to Harry than the revelation about Hoare, because it involved somebody whom he had seen as a trusted role model—and because it would later trigger an even more scandalous tale involving Harry himself.

James Hewitt, his former riding instructor, was directly involved with the October 1994 publication of a book called *Princess in Love*. It was a flowery account of his affair with Harry's mother—a romance that lasted half a decade and had begun when Harry was still in diapers (or "nappies," as they're called in England).

Hewitt had been a regular at Kensington Palace for a long as Harry could remember. The handsome Guards officer, an avid horseman, was hired in the summer of 1986 to teach Diana, and later the boys, to ride. He often visited them at the palace, where he dined with the three of them— as if they were a family. At this point Charles was living at Highgrove, and Harry most likely saw Hewitt on a more regular basis than he did his own father.

Harry, who adores riding horses and took to the sport with his usual athletic flair, had a lot in common with the jovial russet-haired Hewitt— including his looks. Long after the man had faded from Harry's life, cruel rumors would spread that Hewitt, and not Prince Charles, had fathered Diana's second son.

Pure gossip—and impossible gossip, at that. After all, Diana had never even met Hewitt until Harry was a year old.

Yet the accusations, ridiculous as they were, must have wounded Harry deeply. No matter what the tabloids reported about his father's reaction to his birth, no matter how they wanted to portray him as a cold, uncaring father, Harry shares an especially affectionate, openly loving relationship with Charles, whom he affectionately calls Papa.

Although there was no truth to the rumor that

Hewitt was Harry's father, there was certainly truth to the one about the riding instructor's love affair with Harry's mother. Diana herself admitted it in a televised interview in 1995.

But back in 1994, when the book was published, Diana again showed up at Ludgrove to prepare her sons for the whirlwind of tabloid coverage. The boys must have noticed that she didn't officially speak out to deny the fact that she'd had an affair with Hewitt.

But then, Harry must have been weary of having his family's dirty linens aired in public. Much as he seemed to take the constant coverage in stride, he had to be tormented by the hounding.

Revealing video footage of the young prince crossing a beach to take a dip in the sea shows the extent of what Harry had to put up with. Wearing only swim trunks, the boy gamely makes his way across the hot sand—past a row of openly gawking bystanders lined up as though they're standing curbside at a parade.

Harry seems to be doing his best to look straight ahead and appear unfazed as people stare, point, and snap pictures of him. But consider that even an adult would feel uncomfortable under such scrutiny. For a sensitive young boy, who undoubtedly wanted what every other child wants—to fit in and be "normal," one of the crowd—it must have been, and must continue to be, pure agony.

Of course, Diana was tortured by the press, whose relentless stalking tragically led to her death. And William, while he puts up with his share of photo-ops, is just as often likely to glower at the cameras, or duck his head in a refusal to be captured on film.

Harry, meanwhile, seems to take the photographers in stride for the most part. Like his father, who appears to accept the more unpleasant facts of royal life more readily than Diana or William ever have, Harry usually shrugs off the constant flashing of cameras in his face. To his credit, "Harry just doesn't give a damn," observes royal photographer Ken Goff.

While Charles can usually be counted on, in royal tradition, to keep his mouth shut in public about private family business, he broke with custom in 1994 when he cooperated with Jonathan Dimbleby, the author of the book *The Prince of Wales: A Biography*.

In its pages, Harry's father is portrayed as the victim of both his cruelly detached parents and his unstable wife, whom he maintained that he had never loved. The biography was excerpted in the *Sunday London Times* that October, just weeks after Hewitt's embarrassingly tell-all book hit print.

Again, Harry was visited at Ludgrove by his mother. Diana tried to reassure him and William the best she could in light of the disastrous circumstances. Even the royal family was in an uproar over the book. Charles's parents were furious at their son's blatant betrayal.

A former faculty member at the school was quoted as saying at the time, "William and Harry know everything that's going on. The other boys can't resist teasing them about it, and it's impossible to keep them from smuggling the tabloids into the school."

At least their mother was trying to keep a lower profile. Now that Diana was officially "retired," she made fewer official monarchic engagements—and eliminated her security guards, against the advice of the other royals.

Whenever William and Harry were with their mother, they were, as always, accompanied by a full security detail. They had no choice about the matter.

Yet both boys longed for the freedom their mother so fervently sought—and was tragically, ultimately denied. It wasn't easy to fit in at school when your every move was shadowed by a bodyguard, your every conversation in earshot of the vigilant men who eavesdropped out of duty and necessity.

At Ludgrove, nonetheless, the security wasn't as stifling as it might have been. The school's remote location made it relatively safe, and the boys had as much flexibility there as they are likely to ever find anywhere else in their lives.

William and Harry, together at boarding school, until 1995, continued to support each other through each new development in the family drama. But finally the time came for William, at thirteen, to move on.

The September Harry turned eleven he was left behind, not for the first time in his young life, when his older brother completed his studies at Ludgrove and passed the incredibly difficult entrance exams for Eton College.

It isn't a "college" in the American sense—rather, it's the British equivalent of a high school. Located in Windsor on the banks of the River Thames, Eton is attended by more than 1,200 young men—most of them from wealthy families. Harry's maternal grandfather and his uncle had both graduated from the school, as had many members of the royal family, including Princess Margaret's former husband, Lord Snowdon.

The Eton uniform is unique and quaintly old-fashioned—a black coat with tails, a vest, pin-striped dress pants, a stiff-collared white shirt, and shiny black shoes.

Although the schedule is rigid and the academics are challenging, life at this nearly six-centuries-old institution is more inviting, in many ways, than it is at other boarding schools of similar stature. At Eton, comradery is encouraged among the boys, and the school's dorm masters and matrons have an almost parental concern for the students. Presumably, whenever the royal family landed in the press, William—and later, Harry—would be protected by, rather than from, Eton classmates.

Two months after Harry began his solo career at Ludgrove, his mother paid one of her now-customary visits to warm him. This time, it was because she had cone an about-to-be televised interview with British journalist Martin Bashir—an interview that would forever change the way the world viewed Diana and the royal family. Never before had a princess looked a reporter in the eye, on camera, and dropped one bombshell after another as Diana did that fall of 1995.

She conducted the top-secret interview at Kensington Palace without the knowledge of Charles, the queen, or the rest of the family. They found out with the rest of the world on Charles's birthday, November 14, when the interview was announced. It was aired in Britain on November

20. It's doubtful that Harry, away at Ludgrove, where television was prohibited, saw it then, and questionable whether he ever has.

The princess revealed details about her bulimia, her disastrous marriage to Charles, his affair with Camilla Parker Bowles, and her affair with James Hewitt, whom she said she "adored." She also repeatedly discussed her "boys," leaving no doubt that they were her first priority, or that she intended to play an equal role in their upbringing.

The royal divorce, which had until now been stalled, went full speed ahead on the queen's orders. Clearly, she wanted to be rid of the troubled—and troublemaking—Diana, and the sooner the better.

An agreement was hammered out over the next few months. A lump alimony sum was agreed upon, to be paid in installments, and Diana was allowed to stay on at Kensington Palace, mostly so that William and Harry wouldn't have to be uprooted. She did have to give up her royal title—being known as Her Royal Highness. Now she would merely be Diana, Princess of Wales. This might seem like no big deal to someone outside the royal circle, but it basically meant that Harry's mother was formally banished from the royal family.

Mercifully for Harry, there was never a custody

battle, something his mother deeply feared. After all, British law would have given custody to Charles, as William and Harry were the heirs to the throne. It was agreed that Charles and Diana were to share equal custody of the children. Nobody—not the boys' parents, and not the queen, who had final say—wanted to put them through a painful, public tug-of-war.

Harry's parents filed for divorce on July 15, 1996, and it became final on August 28, just before he turned twelve. A new phase of his life had officially begun, with both his parents single and dating. He couldn't know that his mother's life would end almost exactly a year from the fateful day that her marriage ended.

Harry spent a considerable amount of time with his mother during the last two years they had together—as much time as his education, the custody agreement, and her schedule would allow. As busy as she was, Diana's life revolved around her sons.

Because Harry attended an all-boys boarding school, and because he doesn't have a sister, his relationship with his mother played a crucial role in determining how he views and interacts with the opposite sex.

Diana smothered the baby of the family with kisses and hugs, desperately wanting to give him the maternal affection she had longed for herself.

As a result, Harry is an affectionate boy. He was often seen embracing his mother in public, and even now, as a teenager, he isn't afraid to kiss and hug his father in full view of anyone who happens to be watching. Most teenage boys are self-conscious about such behavior, but not Harry. Thanks to his adoring mother, he's comfortable displaying his feelings—something that will serve him well in romantic relationships.

The last time Harry was ever together with both his parents in public was when William was confirmed on March 9, 1997. For the first time in years, they traveled as a family of four, arriving together at St. George's Chapel in Windsor. Charles and Diana seemed to be getting along, even if it was only for the sake of the boys, and everyone was relaxed now that the long years of turmoil over the separation and divorce were behind them.

As a mother, Diana did her best to spend time alone with each of her boys, nurturing them in different ways. Just as she did her best to prepare William to become heir to the throne, she made sure that Harry felt equally loved and important. Her friend Carolyn Bartholomew said that she was "very responsible and responsive to their individual natures, and aware of their character differences."

On June 22, 1997, on a rainy afternoon in London, Harry went with his mother and William to see the Brad Pitt film *The Devil's Own*. This outing caused a huge uproar in the press, not just because the film's rating meant Harry was underage, but because it dealt with the politically explosive IRA.

So even one of his last public appearances with his mother—a seemingly innocent trip to the movies—meant a major controversy. Harry's life was, as always, complicated by the press. But he had not idea that the media would, before summer's end, play a role in—and to some extent, be blamed for—the worst imaginable tragedy to befall him.

Now that Harry was getting older, his father—who had been inexperienced with babies and toddlers, and somewhat hesitant when the boys were young—was more comfortable interacting with him. After the divorce, Charles did his best to keep his sons happy and was involved in their lives as much as he could be.

He introduced Harry to his own passions: art, classical theater, gardening, and, of course, hunting, shooting, and fishing. Like his father, Harry loves stomping around the woods in boots with the royal dogs, an assortment of corgis, Irish setters, Labrador retrievers, and golden retrievers. He particularly enjoyed shooting at rabbits and grouse—something that might seem barbaric to some Americans, but is an enormously important and traditional part of the English royal culture.

Yet even in his newly open, hands-on relationship with Harry, Charles held back one important element—he kept his girlfriend, Camilla, fully out of the picture.

Parker Bowles divorced her husband in 1995, and from that point on, Camilla was constantly with Charles at Highgrove when the boys weren't there. She acted as hostess when she and Charles entertained, drove his car, and lived with him as though they were married. But Charles made sure that whenever William and Harry came on the scene, Camilla disappeared. He was determined that his precious time with his sons was to be devoted to them alone.

Diana doesn't seem to have been quite as discreet about her own relationships. She occasionally introduced her sons to men she was dating. Among them was Will Carling, the married captain of the English rugby team. Harry, as a sports fan, looked up to Carling as a hero, and probably didn't question the nature of his mother's relationship with the man, whose wife would later claim Diana broke up their marriage.

But the romance between Diana and Will Carling was fairly short-lived. She spent much of the last year of her life involved with a Pakistani heart surgeon, Hasnat Khan.

Still, despite her many friends, would-be suitors, and her charity work—the latest on behalf of victims of land mines—Diana was as lonely as ever and depressed. It was Harry who saved the day on her thirty-sixth birthday, July 1, 1997—the last birthday she would ever have. Perhaps instinctively knowing his mother needed to be cheered up, he called her and sang "Happy Birthday" over the phone, joined by a crowd of his school friends.

Less than two weeks later, Harry joined his mother and William for their annual summer vacation together.

This year, they were going to the south of France, where they had been invited to be guests at the seaside Saint Tropez estate of Mohamed Al Fayed. The controversial Egyptian-born businessman, who owned Harrods in London, one of Diana's favorite department stores, had often invited Diana and the boys to visit. Diana had always turned him down, perhaps because the royal family wasn't crazy about the outspoken—even boorish—Fayed.

This time, though, Diana accepted his invitation—primarily because she craved privacy for her vacation with Harry and William. Fayed's enormous wealth was able to provide that, to an extent.

At Fayed's seaside compound, Harry, his mother, and his brother were shown to a private guest house with its own pool and full staff of servants.

Security was heavy. Fayed employed a full squad of armed guards. Harry, in addition to his usual bodyguard, was assigned to his own Scotland Yard detective.

Despite the ever-present reminder that his every move was under surveillance, Harry frolicked and played. He donned a life jacket and jet-skied—often with his mother as his laughing passenger. He swam, sailed on Fayed's yacht, the *Jonikal*, rode bumper cars at an amusement park, and enjoyed an elaborate Bastille Day fireworks display. And after months of boarding-school food, the growing soon-to-be-teenage boy gorged himself on ice cream, lobster, and soft drinks.

Harry and William were also treated to two nights at a nearby disco. The place had been rented out just for them by Dodi Al Fayed, Mohamed's forty-two-year old son.

Harry's mother was captivated by Dodi, a Hollywood producer and internationally known playboy. The boys appeared to be congenial with him, too, and he taught them to water-ski, much to athletic Harry's delight.

After spending a little more than a week at the Fayed compound, Harry returned to London with his mother and brother.

Dodi promptly sent dozens of pink roses, enough to fill the whole apartment with their sweet scent. It's easy to imagine plucky Harry teasing Diana about it. He loved to joke with his mother, even calling her "Squidgy" after the embarrassing tape has been released to the press years earlier.

Harry and William dutifully and politely wrote thank-you notes to Fayed—their mother had trained them well. Meanwhile, Diana flew to Milan on July 22 to attend a memorial service for her friend Gianni Versace, the clothing designer.

The flamboyant Italian had been murdered days before by a serial killer in Miami, Florida, for no other reason than his fame had captivated the madman's attention. The horrific crime had severely shaken Diana, who always worried about the safety of her children, living in the public eye as they did. It was a grim reminder that life in the public eye bears more than it share of perils.

She sat beside her friend Elton John at the memorial service, and they were photographed leaning on each other for support. The two of them had been arguing recently, and they had all but cut off their longtime relationship. The tragic loss of their friend brought them together again, and this set the stage for what was to become one of the most poignant moments at Diana's own funeral six weeks later.

After the Versace service, Diana again left the boys at Kensington Palace and flew to Paris with Dodi for a few days, officially launching their romance for all the world to see.

One of Diana's friends would later say in an interview that while William was unhappy about his mother's new romance, the more upbeat, relaxed Harry didn't really mind it.

Meanwhile, Harry, on summer break from school, had little to do. Cooped up in the castle apartment, with his mother distracted by her new boyfriend, the lively prince couldn't wait to get to Balmoral, where he would spend the rest of the summer outdoors. Luckily for him, Diana agreed that he and William could leave earlier than scheduled for Scotland.

As he kissed and hugged his mother good-bye that July day, Harry had no idea it was for the last time.

He was eager to start the next phase of his vacation, and to see his beloved father. And he didn't even have to worry about his mother being lonely, for a change. She was giddy and excited about her latest romance.

At Balmoral, Harry got right down to business. He desperately wanted to be "blooded"—that is, to shoot his first stag and wear a smear of its blood on his face for everyone to see. It was an age-old English rite of passage—one William had reached the year before. As always, Harry was eager to catch up with his big brother, and he spent much of that August in Scotland determinedly stalking stags with his rifle slung over his shoulder.

During an official photo session a few weeks after his arrival in Balmoral, Harry appeared chipper and content. Climbing on a rocky stream bank amid lush greenery, he was dressed in khaki-colored pleated corduroy pants, a white dress shirt with the sleeves rolled up, and brown leather shoes—more casually than his kilt-clad father, but not nearly as relaxed as his wardrobe had been on vacation with his mother in July.

But that was the norm for him—taking on one style to suit the royal family, and another with his more laid-back mother.

Surprisingly, he appears equally comfortable in dress slacks and shirt or in jeans and sneakers. He does seem to have developed his own sense of style as early as 1995, as seen in a photo session of him, William, Beatrice, and Eugenie on the ski slopes at Kloster in Switzerland, a favorite resort of the royal family. Harry, unlike the others, rakishly wears a bandanna around his head.

That August of 1997 at Balmoral, Harry spent time with Tiggy Legge-Bourke. The nanny no longer worked for his father—in part because his mother resented her. Diana never could get past her jealousy of Tiggy, to the point where Charles obviously felt it was best to eliminate the controversy from their already stressed lives.

Besides, at twelve and fifteen, the princes were a bit old to need official child care at that point. But that doesn't mean they weren't still crazy about Tiggy.

To Harry, she was like a big sister. A few days before his mother's death, the two of them—Tiggy in trousers tucked into boots, Harry in a camouflage jacket with a jaunty cap on his head, both clutching rifles and ammunition—trekked through the woods together, hunting.

Meanwhile, on August 14, his mother had left for a Greek cruise with a female friend, who later told the press that when they visited a church along the way, Diana lit candles for each of her sons and talked openly about her love for them. She also called them at Balmoral nearly every day—even from her cell phone the week of August 21, when she was cruising the Mediterranean with Dodi aboard the *Jonikal*.

By then, her relationship with the international playboy was splashed in living color across the pages of magazines and newspapers around the world. Gossip had it that they were discussing marriage. But while the stories were largely backed by those attached to Fayed, they were—at the time, and later—denied by most who were close to Diana.

By Thursday, August 28, Harry's vacation was winding down. Now he was looking forward to seeing his mother again. Diana was, that day, on Dodi's yacht moored off the Sardinian coast. That night, Harry and William attended the annual Ghillies Ball. The lively event was hosted by the queen for her Balmoral staff and the local people. For the occasion Harry wore his kilt, and he danced with fun-loving Tiggy, who was invited.

One Friday, the last day of her shipboard vacation, Diana spoke to Mohamed Al Fayed by telephone. She told the owner of Harrods that the first thing she planned to do back in London the coming week was visit the store and buy some birthday presents for Harry.

September 15 would, after all, mark an important milestone in his life: He would become a

Harry's christening

Baby Harry held by Mummy Diana

Toddler Harry dressed all in blue

Dressing just like William

Hanging out with big brother Wills

Attending a polo match with Charles

A day out with Diana

At Eton college with Charles, Diana and William

On the soccer field

On vacation in Switzerland

Shy Harry

In uniform the first day at Eton

Hitting the ski slopes in Switzerland

Looking at the floral tributes to Mummy

Smiling for the camera

Handsome Harry

teenager on that day. Fun-loving Harry had asked his mother for a computer-game system as one of his gifts.

On Saturday, August 30, Diana and Dodi flew from Sardinia to Paris, where they were going to spend the night. Meanwhile, back at Balmoral, Harry's bags were being packed for his return to London the next day.

He was looking forward to seeing his mother again, but not necessarily to going back to school. He wouldn't be joining his brother at Eton as he had hoped. His grades weren't what they should be, and his parents decided that he needed to be held back at Ludgrove for another year.

Although Charles and Diana felt it was for the best, and Harry would be returning to familiar territory, they had no way of knowing that when September did come, he would be in need of his older brother's support more than ever. But he was destined to tough it alone for another year, trying his best to raise his grades so that he could follow in his older brother's footsteps once again.

While in Paris, according to *The Day Diana Died*, by Christopher Andersen, Diana had fully intended to shop for gifts for her younger son's birthday. But with the press swarming all over her the moment she landed, she knew that would be impossible. So she sent an employee of the Ritz hotel, which was owned by Dodi's father, to pick up the presents she needed. One of them was the computer play station Harry wanted.

Andersen's book also mentions a phone call made by Prince William to his mother on the last night of her life. William was worried that an upcoming photo session he was to do at Eton would overshadow Harry, who would be back at Ludgrove. Both William and Diana were sensitive to the fact that Harry was often bypassed—particularly in the press—in favor of the heir of the throne.

Regardless of whether the details of this phone call are true, there is no doubt that Diana's mind was on her children that night as she dined with Dodi at the Ritz.

Or that, hundreds of miles away in Scotland, Harry's thoughts settled on tomorrow's reunion with his mother as he lay in bed just before ten that night in the room adjoining his brother's, drifting off to a peaceful slumber for the last time in the foreseeable future.

Grieving Mummy

Losing a beloved parent at any age is difficult, but when you're a child or teenager, still needing your mother or father's daily guidance and reassurance, it can be devastating.

How did Harry cope with his overwhelming loss? How does anyone his age survive losing their mother?

When a death is sudden, as Diana's was, there is no time to prepare yourself for the impact. You go into a state of shock, and it serves to protect the body, in a sense, from the full brunt of the pain. During those first few days at Balmoral, when Harry was isolated with William and his family, he hadn't yet absorbed the loss and maybe didn't entirely believe it, either.

He was most likely still dazed when he managed to walk behind her coffin in the funeral procession. Though he shed many tears during the first week after Diana's death, perhaps the most difficult time still lay ahead. After the funeral, as the initial shock wore off and the rhythm of his life became more normal, it began to sink in that Diana really was gone forever.

By all accounts, Harry bore his pain courageously, not dwelling on it or speaking much about it to schoolmates. According to Dr. Benjamin Garber, a Chicago psychiatrist specializing in children's bereavement who was quoted in a *People* magazine article about Diana's sons in mourning, "the main thing adolescents do is try not to show their feelings about loss."

Thus, outwardly, as during his South Africa visit two months after his mother died, Harry was often smiling and appeared carefree. There was little evidence that he was still torn up inside, still trying to adapt to life without the mother who had always showered him with love and shielded him from hurt.

Everywhere he turned, there were reminders of his mother's death—not just in his personal life, but in newspapers and magazines, on television, and in the crowds that gathered during his public appearances, wanting to offer their sympathy. As time goes by, the attention has faded, but it will probably never truly be erased. Harry will forever be shadowed by the trauma of losing his mother. Yet, with time come acceptance, peace, and the knowledge that he isn't alone.

Psychiatrist Dennis Friedman, author of *Inheritance: A Psychological History of the Royal Family*, noted about Harry and his older brother that "as time goes on, they will be comforted to know that the country is grieving with them. It's not a huge comfort, but it helps."

CHAPTER 7

Good-bye Mummy

Life at Balmoral may have been more casual than at Buckingham Palace, but Harry's time there was definitely scheduled. Sunday mornings were always spent attending the eleven o'clock service at the small local church called Crathie Kirk.

There are conflicting reports on how, exactly, Harry started this particular Sunday morning. Some accounts have Prince Charles waking him and William; others have Charles waiting until the boys had awakened on their own. Some have Prince Charles sitting the boys down together; others have him talking alone to William first, and the two of them then confronting Harry together.

What is agreed upon, however, is that some time around seven-thirty on the morning of August 31, Harry saw pain in his father's eyes and heard anguish in his voice, and he knew, with a sick feeling of dread in the moments before the bombshell was dropped, that something traumatic had occurred.

Gently Charles told Harry that while he had been asleep, his beloved Mummy had been killed in a car accident in Paris, along with Dodi Fayed and their driver, Henri Paul.

Thankfully, there are no eyewitnesses to this intensely personal, private moment between father and son—of, if there are, those who were there have kept the details to themselves out of respect for the child who had suffered the worst loss imaginable.

It goes without saying that Harry's reaction was one of shock and intense grief.

It goes without saying that he shed tears and was comforted by his father.

It goes without saying that he realized on that grim, awful morning that his life had been changed forever.

Rather than remaining inside the castle to grieve away from the prying eyes of strangers, Harry, along with William and Charles, joined the rest of the royal family for church services a few hours later. There has been speculation that the queen or Charles ordered them to attend, but it is just as likely that the boys made up their minds on their own.

In any case, they put on their Sunday best and climbed into the backseat of a car with their kilt-clad father sitting between them. They were driven to Crathie Kirk. The ever-present photographers mercilessly snapped photos of them behind the glass, as though they were animals on display at a zoo.

In those stark, heart-wrenching pictures, Harry sits staring straight ahead, his eyes dry but swollen, his jaw set firmly as if to keep it from trembling. His father and William are similarly positioned, their hands clasped in their laps, gazes focused blankly in front of them.

Nobody knows what was going through Harry's mind. But he had to be longing for the embrace of his mother, who had, until now, always been there to put her arms around him and comfort him in troubled times.

Now she was gone, and he was desperately in need of solace.

At the church Harry sat stoically through a regular service. No mention was made of his mother. According to one published account, Harry, perplexed by this, turned to his father and asked in disbelief, "Are you sure Mummy is dead?"

Yes, Diana was dead, and the fact that she wasn't mentioned is brutal testimony to the fact that the divorce had cast her firmly out of the royal family. She was no longer one of them.

But Harry and William, her own flesh and blood, still belonged.

The bereaved "Heir" and "Spare" were forced in their time of need to lean on the very people who had made their mother's life miserable for years, from Charles to his parents to Tiggy Legge-Bourke.

There is no evidence that the newly motherless boys were treated in anything but the most kind and sensitive manner. From that day on, Charles seems to have taken on a new aura of paternal tenderness. He appeared to be doing everything within his power to ease his children through the darkest days of their lives, and he seldom seems to have left their side.

However, he did have to travel to Paris to bring Diana's body back home that afternoon, and he was determined to spare Harry and William that ordeal.

His actions that day as he accompanied his former wife on her final journey back to England were meant to show that despite the bitter divorce, Charles now felt nothing but respect and grief toward the woman who had borne him two sons.

Symbolically, in going to Paris and bringing her home, he was showing the world that despite the way she had been erased from his family, their bond had never been entirely broken.

There's no doubt that it's what his sons wanted him to do—that both Harry and William felt it was proper for their father to bring their mother home. But there were many who simply didn't see it that way. Some people felt that Charles had overstepped his bounds—by divorcing Diana, he had relinquished his role in her life and her death.

He simply couldn't win. If he hadn't gone to Paris, he most certainly would have been condemned in the press. But he most likely did what he did for his boys, and they—most likely—were grateful.

After the church service that Sunday morning, Harry was driven back to Balmoral with William and the rest of the family. Meanwhile, Charles, accompanied by Diana's sisters, Jane and Sarah, boarded a plane for France.

Televisions around the world showed live coverage of the unfolding story.

Nobody knows whether William and Harry watched, along with millions of others, as their mother's casket, draped in the Royal Standard, was ceremoniously transported, accompanied by the Queen's Color Squadron of the RAF Regiment, various dignitaries, their father, and their aunts.

Again there are conflicting accounts. Some say the boys did witness the event on television; others say that the queen had banned television, radios, and even newspapers from Balmoral to shield her grandsons from the worldwide hysteria.

Tiggy, who had been immediately summoned by Prince Charles, showed up at Balmoral that day. There is no doubt that Harry was glad to see her. Though he would become a teenager in only two weeks, on that Sunday afternoon he was a devastated little boy who had just lost his beloved mother. He desperately needed reassuring hugs and an attentive ear, and it's highly unlikely he received them from his grandmother.

Though the boys reportedly call the queen by the affectionate-sounding nickname "Granny," she isn't exactly known for showering them with kisses and love as so many grannies do their grandchildren. Harry was unlikely to curl up on her lap to have a good cry, although he must have done so with more maternal, outwardly caring Tiggy.

Somehow Harry, comforted by Tiggy and William, managed to get through those terrible hours as the news sank in. Charles, who had promised to get back to Balmoral as soon as he possibly could, did so early that evening. Meanwhile, Diana's body was brought to St. James's Palace in London, where it lay in state at the Chapel Royal.

The days that followed were incredibly difficult for Harry. As reporters around the world converged on London, he remained with his royal family in seclusion at Balmoral. Though he did his best to keep up a brave front in the royal tradition, at times he was quite simply inconsolable.

According to *William: The Inside Story of the Man Who Will Be King*, by Nicholas Davies, Harry spent the first few days frequently in tears, repeating over and over, "Why? Why did she die?" He underwent a dramatic personality change, suddenly willing to agree to whatever decisions his older brother made about how things were to be handled.

Ordinarily, feisty, strong-willed Harry didn't hesitate to voice his opinions and rarely consulted others about decisions.

Though the world grieved and sympathy was showered upon Harry and William from every direction, they were, in effect, isolated in their sorrow. Once again, the two young brothers were united in an ordeal they alone understood. Once again, they turned to each other for support.

Davies's book credits William with helping Harry get through the rough period. His protective big-brother instinct kicked in, and William was at Harry's side almost constantly, the two of them often arm in arm. With Tiggy, the bereft princes halfheartedly played games, went for walks, and kicked a football around outside—anything to stay busy.

Whenever Harry's anguish spilled over, William urged him to think only of the wonderful times they'd had with their mother.

During the days Harry put on a brave front the best he could; it was the nights that were the hardest. When darkness fell, he knew he had to crawl into his lonely bed and confront the full force of his grief.

William, perhaps sensing what his mother would have wanted him to do, stayed up with his little brother at night, as Diana had when Harry was younger and sick or troubled. William didn't go to bed himself, until he knew Harry was safely asleep.

On Tuesday, September 2, Harry's aunts—his mother's sisters, Lady Jane Fellowes and Sarah McCorquodale—and his uncle, Diana's brother, Charles, Earl Spencer, arrived at Balmoral. For the first time in years, the royal family and the Spencer family came together with a single purpose: to ease the tremendous pain of William and Harry and to plan a suitable farewell for their mother.

Outside the gates of Balmoral, mourners were gathering and laying bouquets of flowers, notes of sympathy, poems, and other tributes to Harry's mother.

Inside, funeral plans were being made for

Diana, who, now that she was no longer a part of the royal family, was no longer entitled to a state funeral. Charles involved not just the royal family, the Spencer family, and Tony Blair, Britain's new prime minister, but also Harry and William.

The boys wanted their mother to be remembered in death for the things she cared about during her life. So when the list of invitations was drawn up, it included not just British and foreign dignitaries and heads of state, but also the ordinary people Diana had touched in her life. There were, in addition to her many friends, representatives of the many charities she had patronized—people who were homeless, or dying of AIDS, or maimed by land mines.

London was already jammed with mourners who had made the pilgrimage to say good-bye to a woman who had captivated the entire world. Kensington Palace, where she had lived, was now surrounded not just be gates meant to keep the commoners out but by the sea of blossoms the commoners had brought to honor their beloved Diana.

Although since the divorce she was no longer Britain's princess, Diana was clearly—as she had wished to be—"the People's Princess."

The media was awash with images from London—and scenes of the Paris tunnel where Harry's mother had died.

As me and more details emerged, it became clear that the Mercedes in which Diana and Dodi were riding was trying to outrun reporters who were tailing it. Henri Paul, the driver, was legally intoxicated and driving at a high rate of speed.

But the widespread sentiment was that the blame lay squarely with the tabloid press that had hounded the royal family, especially Diana, for years.

It was no secret—privately or publicly—that Diana resented, even loathed, the tabloid journalists who made her life "hell," in her own words. In his profound sorrow over his mother's death, Harry couldn't help but bear anger toward the media he had always tolerated so much more willingly than his mother or William.

Anger is a natural part of grieving, but in time it tends to subside. Harry's recent encounters with the press seem to prove that he has come to terms with the role the reporters and photographers played in Diana's death. He continues to put up bravely with the media coverage of his life.

The first true test of his courage came on Friday, September 5, when, after five days of seclusion, Harry flew back to London with his father, William, and Tiggy.

The boys went first to Kensington Palace,

where they confronted their grief all over again as they stepped into the home they had shared with their mother. Diana's presence was everywhere, and so were the awful reminders that Harry would never again sit across from her at the table, climb into her bed to cuddle with her, or romp playfully through the rooms, teasing her.

Somehow he managed to compose himself to make a public appearance with his father and William outside the palace. The crowds, which were gathered behind the barriers that had been set up at the gates, had no idea they were coming, and there was an enormous, spontaneous out-pouring of emotion and sympathy when the boys appeared.

Harry, dressed somberly in a dark suit and tie, clung tightly to his protective father with one hand and stretched his other to clasp the hands of the hundreds of people reaching out to him, call-ing out their condolences, sobbing, letting Harry know how very much they cared. He bent over from time to time to read notes that had been left admidst the bouquets, and he thanked people repeatedly, politely, somehow maintaining his decorum.

His brave front would again be called into duty the following morning. Harry and William had decided that they wanted to walk the mile from

St. James's Palace, where they were staying with their father, to Westminster Abbey, where the funeral was to be held.

It hadn't been an easy decision. It would mean being on display not just for the throngs that would line the route and the cameras that would broadcast the image around the world, but also that they would have to follow their mother's coffin, the most vivid reminder that she was gone forever.

But Harry would do it for his mother. He would do anything for his mother.

That Friday night, Queen Elizabeth addressed her public in a televised address that began, "What I say to you now as your Queen and as a grandmother, I say from my heart."

As her words were broadcast through the grieving nation, people generally were thinking, *It's about time.* The press had berated the queen for her conspicuous absence in her grief-stricken hometown and for her silence on the death of a daughter-in-law whom she had ultimately seen as a problem that would have to be eliminated.

Now she did everything in her power to restore her image, saying, "First, I want to pay tribute to Diana, myself. She was an exceptional and gifted human being. In good times and in bad, she never lost her capacity to smile and laugh, to inspire others with her warmth and kindness. I admired and respected her for her energy and commitment to others, especially for her devotion to her two boys."

The next morning, dressed again in a dark suit and tie, his hair neatly combed forward, Harry waited with his brother, his father, his uncle Earl Spencer, and his grandfather, Prince Philip, at St. James's Palace.

Meanwhile, his mother's coffin was being transported on an antique gun carriage through the streets, pulled by six horses of the King's Troop Royal Horse Artillery and surrounded by uniformed Welsh Guards.

Harry himself offered the most poignant symbol of that grim day. In a place of honor on top of the flag-draped casket was a wreath of fragrant white roses topped by a card upon which he had written, "Mummy."

Marching behind the casket were more than five hundred representatives of Diana's charities. Some were in wheelchairs and on crutches, stark reminders of the way the princess had reached out to those who were suffering, doing her best to ease their pain.

Just before the cortege was to pass Buckingham Palace, the gates opened and the entire royal family emerged. There was a murmuring of surprise in the crowd.

Sentiments were not running in favor of the

royal family after a week in which the queen's silence on her former daughter-in-law's death was followed by finally lowering the palace flag to half-mast, and a public address that seemed to be too little, too late.

So when Harry's grandparents, aunts, uncles, and cousins emerged in a show of solidarity to bow their heads in respect to his mother's casket, there was an enormous sense of public relief. The family had stood by Harry and William.

As the coffin approached the spot where Harry stood, he felt thousands of pairs of eyes on him, and he heard the anguished sobs and wails in the crowd of mourners that stood twenty deep along the street.

Yet he kept his head up and his arms stiff at his side as he fell into step behind it. His shoulders were hunched, as if with the tremendous effort to contain his emotions. On his left was his father; on his right his uncle—the two men a protective presence, yet, unable to put their arms around Harry to help him through this ordeal.

Nobody could. He had to do this alone, for Mummy.

Somehow, he made it through. Somehow, he held back the flood of tears.

Looking straight ahead, unlike William, who for the most part kept his blond head bowed, Harry marched with the valor of a true soldier in that solemn procession to the packed Westminster Abbey.

There, in a service led by the Archbishop of Canterbury, the Most Reverend George Carey, Diana was prayed for and remembered. Her favorite hymns were sung. Her two sisters read poems. Earl Spencer gave the eulogy.

It was a memorable speech, during which he lashed out not just at the press he blamed for Diana's death, but at the royal family itself. He made it clear that Harry and William would not be encompassed by the Windsors, now that their mother was gone.

Addressing Diana, he said, "I pledge that we, your blood family, will do all we can to continue the imaginative and loving way in which you were steering these two exceptional young men so that their souls are not simply immersed by duty and tradition but can sing openly, as you planned. We fully respect the heritage into which they have both been born, and will always respect and encourage them in their royal role. But we, like you, recognize the need for them to experience as many different aspects of life as possible, to arm them spiritually and emotionally for the years ahead."

Turning directly to Diana's two children, he said, speaking for himself and for people around the world, "William and Harry, we all care desperately for you today. We are all chewed up with sadness at the loss of a woman who wasn't even our mother. How great your suffering is we cannot even imagine."

Thankfully, the cameras inside the Abbey were not allowed to film Harry's face during the service.

Later, there would be reports from those who had witnessed the service that both he and William had applauded their uncle's remarks, along with the rest of the congregation and the throngs of mourners on the streets outside, where the service was televised on enormous screens.

Their father and his parents did not applaud.

Eyewitnesses inside the Abbey noted, too, that Harry had maintained his composure during all but one portion of the service.

Harry reportedly broke down in sobs when his mother's friend Elton John sat at the piano and sang "Goodbye, England's Rose," a version of his hit "Candle in the Wind" that he had hastily composed that week just for Diana.

It was over.

All that remained was for Harry to ride with his father, brother, and his mother's family the eighty miles by train to Althorp, where Diana was to be buried.

Her brother had chosen to place her grave on a serene little island in the middle of a scenic lake on the grounds of the estate. There, he reasoned, Harry and his brother could visit their mother in privacy, away from cameras and strangers' prying eyes.

Aside from the intimate group of mourners and the vicar from the local church, there were no witnesses to the burial. Only those who had loved her most watched as Diana's casket was lowered into the ground.

The grave was scattered with flowers from the sixty million blossoms left by mourners in London.

There, they would scatter their seed and cover the little island with fragrant blooms in years to come.

Second Sons

"The Spare" isn't the most flattering thing a boy can be called at birth, but Harry wasn't the first little boy who was ever born in the shadow of an older brother. Still, Harry is part of the royal family, which means that the differences between him and William are more extreme than in a typical family with two sons.

William will inherit a throne, a vast empire, and tremendous wealth.

Harry's main role is to stand by in case something happens to William between now and the time when William has a child of his own, who will then be next in line for the throne, bumping Harry back in order.

Best-selling author Dr. Kevin Leman, an internationally known psychologist, has done considerable research on sibling relationships. In *The New Birth Order Book,* he writes, "Second-born children develop their own lifestyle, according to the perceptions they have about themselves and the key persons in their lives. Needless to say, that older sibling is a key person in the second born's life."

Often, a second child will deliberately cultivate interests—and even personality traits—that are the total opposite of his older sibling's. This is especially true if the two are close in age. Certainly outgoing, happy-go-lucky, daredevil Harry is a remarkable contrast to the me reserved, solemn, cautious William.

Of course, there are exceptions—in fact as well as in fiction. Look at Frasier and Niles Crane, characters on the hit television sitcom *Frasier.* They're both psychologists, both snobs, both more interested in the arts than athletics—in essence, mirror images of each other!

Frasier and Niles, like Harry and William, and countless other pairs of brothers, are also fairly competitive. According to Leman, "rivalry is most intense when you have a two-child family with two boys. Older brother is going to . . . be the leader, and also the family 'sheriff' or 'policeman,' as far as keeping the younger brother in line. Older brother often finds himself being the protector of baby brother." Meanwhile, "the younger child looks the situation over and usually branches off in a different direction. That different direction may still put him in direct rivalry with his older brother. If he is determined to catch up with him and surpass him as far as leadership and achievement are concerned, this can get sticky."

Harry, although he once teasingly volunteered to take over the throne if William wasn't willing, doesn't seem to genuinely challenge William's lofty status or show designs on overthrowing his brother's birthright. In fact, he seems to respect William's awesome responsibility, and he certainly gets a kick out of William's recent emergence as the family's primary heartthrob.

When it comes to romance, according to Leman, growing up in a two-son family has its drawbacks. "Two brothers have no trouble learning how to interact with peers of their own sex, [however] they tend to have little preparation for interaction with the opposite sex. The relationship between Mom and her two sons is critical. She is the one who has to do all of the teaching and modeling as to what women are really all about."

Of course, Harry had a close and mutually affectionate, respectful relationship with his mother while she was alive. But he lost her when he was on the cusp of adolescence, a difficult time in most boys' lives, when their thoughts are beginning to turn to girls and dating. Not only does Harry no longer have a mother to serve as a role model for interaction with females, but he attends an all-boys boarding school.

Luckily, his relationship with Tiggy has helped him along where women are concerned. And he does have fairly close relationships with female cousins Zara Phillips and Laura Fellowes.

"As important as your child's order of birth may be," Leman points out, "it is only an influence, not a final fact of life forever set in cement and unchangeable as far as how that child will turn out."

William might be destined to be king, but that doesn't mean Harry isn't bound for leadership, as well. In fact, many American presidents were second-born children. Among the many who have older siblings, those who are second sons like Harry include Andrew Johnson, Herbert Hoover, Franklin Roosevelt, John F. Kennedy, Richard Nixon, Ronald Reagan, and George Bush.

Here are a few more of Harry's historic counterparts:

The younger of two sons, the **Prodigal Son** in a New Testament parable [Luke 15:11–32] demanded his share of his inheritance and went away to squander it. When he returned, penniless yet truly repentant, he was welcomed back into his father's house with a joyous celebration.

According to the Old Testament Book of Genesis [4:1–16], **Abel,** a shepherd and the second son of Adam and Eve, was murdered by his older brother, Cain, out of jealousy after God refused Cain's sacrifices and not Abel's.

King Richard I, also known as Richard

the Lion Heart, became first in line for the British throne after his older brother, Henry, died. When his father, King Henry II, died in 1189, he ascended to the throne.

In 1936 Harry's great-grandfather, **King George VI**, the second son of Kind George V, inherited the throne from his older brother, Edward VIII. After ruling for ten months, Edward had abdicated in order to marry the woman he loved, Wallis Simpson, an American divorcée who was deemed unsuitable for the role of queen.

Harry's own uncle and godfather, Charles's younger brother **Prince Andrew,** the Duke of York, is known as much for his good looks and relatively laid-back personality as he is for his failed marriage to Sarah Ferguson and the surrounding scandal in the press.

The aforementioned **John Fitzgerald Kennedy,** who became the thirty-fifth president of the United States, idolized his older brother, Joseph, who as a child vowed to be president one day. When he was tragically killed when his plane went down over England during World War II, John stepped in to fulfill his brother's political ambitions.

Of course, not all second sons are noble— even in the Bible. According to Genesis [25, 27], **Jacob,** the younger son of Isaac and

Rebekah, tricked his older brother, Esau, into selling him his birthright for a bowl of stew, thus cheating him.

Movies, television, and literature are filled with vengeful kid brothers, too. Remember **Scar** in Disney's animated *The Lion King?* He was determined to kill off his ruling brother, Mufasa, and Mufasa's son, Simba, so that he would inherit the throne.

But over all, Prince Harry is in good company—and ready to stake his own claim to fame.

CHAPTER 8

Life without Diana

After the funeral, Harry and William went with their father to Highgrove, where they spent a week with Charles and Tiggy.

Life was hardly back to normal. They should have been back at school by now, settling in to September's familiar rhythm of lessons and textbooks and dormitory rules.

But Harry and William weren't yet ready to face the world. They needed more time to heal, and their father saw that they had it. Together they engaged in familiar, beloved activities against the country backdrop Harry loved so dearly. They also read some of the mail that poured in—a quarter of a million condolences from around the world.

At the end of the week, Charles resumed his schedule, but not without publicly addressing the difficulties the family had endured—and his admiration for the way his young sons had borne their grief. "I am unbelievably proud of the two of them, William and Harry. They are really quite remarkable. I think they have handled a very difficult time with enormous courage and the greatest possible dignity." He went on to add that as difficult as it is for anyone to lose a loved one, "perhaps you might realize it is even harder when the whole world is watching."

There is no doubt that Harry was strengthened by his father's public praise. Charles was not given to emotional outbursts. This was the first public sign that he wasn't the chilly, remote royal father the press had tried to create. His love and affection for his children was evident to all as the tragic events of the past days had played themselves out at center stage.

Now it was time for Harry to return to school. While it helped, in a sense, that he would be going back to familiar territory at Ludgrove rather than embarking on a huge change and starting Eton, he would be forced to go it alone for the first time since his mother's death. William would no longer be at his side, looking out for him the way he had since they had received the devastating news about Diana.

While Ludgrove had strict rules about the students' communication with their families back home, the headmaster agreed that, in light of what Harry was going through, the prince could make calls to and receive calls from William whenever he needed.

At school, Harry quickly settled into a familiar routine of classes, sporting events, and meals with his friends. But he was reportedly quieter than usual, spending more time alone than he ever had in the past.

Mindful of his loss, the staff at the school took extra care of him, doing their best to help him through the terrible transition as he absorbed the full blow of his mother's death. Housemaster Gerald Barber and his wife, Janet, made sure that Harry had support everywhere he turned.

The bleak days passed slowly. It was especially hard on Harry when his thirteenth birthday came and went without the usual fanfare his mother would have made. Harry was a teenager now, but he had officially left childhood behind two weeks earlier, on the dark morning of August 31.

On the bittersweet morning of his birthday, his aunt, Lady Sarah McCorquodale, drove to Ludgrove to give him a special gift—the last he would ever receive from his mother. It was the computer game system Diana had bought for him on the last day of her life.

In the months following his mother's death, Harry found that the press was seeming to keep its distance for a change. It was as though the tabloid reporters were actually heeding his family's request and allowing him to mourn in peace—small comfort considering their role in his loss, but it did help.

As a result, little has been written about how Harry managed to cope during that most painful period in his young life. It's certain that he relied heavily on telephone contact and visits with his father, brother, and Tiggy. Lady Sarah and Diana's older sister, Lady Jane Fellowes, called Harry nearly every day and visited him at school as often as they could.

In fact, his aunt Jane dropped in on him every two weeks or so, to make sure he was coping all right. And his aunt Sarah invited him to spend two weeks of the coming summer on vacation with her and her children in Cornwall, but Harry turned down the invitation. He wanted to be with his father at Balmoral, as he had always spend his summers.

In early November Harry was to have spent his midterm break with his mother. Now, his father hurriedly shuffled his plans in order to have Harry join him on a visit to South Africa to meet with Nelson Mandela.

Harry flew to South Africa with Tiggy and his school friend Charlie Henderson, who was also thirteen. After the three wen on a safari in Botswana, they met up with Harry's father in Johannesburg, where Charles had arranged for the two of them to attend a concert by the British pop group The Spice Girls.

Harry was thrilled, and not just because he was a huge fan of the band. It was very similar to the kind of thing his mother would have done for him. And while Harry didn't show up in the jeans and T-shirt he'd most likely have worn if Diana were accompanying him—he wore a suit and tie instead—he seemed perfectly at ease in his father's company, and very excited to meet the beautiful rock stars he admired.

Backstage after the show, Harry tried to stand aside as his father thanked the band for playing free at the Two Nations concert. But as Charles kissed and thanked each of the girls, they pulled Harry into the action, making a fuss over him as he overcame his initial shyness and grinned broadly at all the female attention, particularly when gorgeous, blond Emma Bunton, known as "Baby Spice," kissed him on the cheek.

When Harry and Charles visited a Zulu school, where they were treated to a traditional dance performed by topless tribal women, the cameras captured Harry's initial embarrassment as he blushed and tried to figure out where he was supposed to be looking. Finally he broke into a broad grin that tickled onlookers.

In a remote settlement called Dukuduku, Harry was amused when Prince Charles agreed to sample the local beer—and wound up with a frothy mustache. Laughing, Harry offered him a handkerchief.

In the city of Durban, Harry again showed his impish side. As Charles shook hands with well-wishers outside City Hall, which was adjacent to the Royal Hotel where they were staying, Harry snuck out onto the balcony with a camera.

The crowds went wild when Harry began snapping pictures of his unsuspecting dad below. Amid shrieks of "Harry, Harry!" Charles grinned and pointed overhead, saying, "He's right there—under the letter H."

Harry had to return to England and school before Charles's scheduled visit to Cape Town, so he was unable to accompany his father in visiting his uncle, Earl Spencer. For all Diana's brother's pledges and promises to assist in his nephews' upbringing, the truth was that Harry didn't see or speak to him very often after his mother's death. He loved his father very much and wanted to be with him, no matter what his mother's family or the rest of the world thought.

Harry had collected countless souvenirs from his vacation, including a large assortment of Zulu shields, spears, and sticks, and a Zulu bracelet he bought for Tiggy. The unprecedented father-son vacation was a smashing success. For the first time ever, Charles seemed to relax a bit in front of the cameras. And Harry, now over the initial shock and grief of his mother's death, actually appeared to have regained a bit of his usual spirit.

Later that month Harry joined the royal family at a gala celebration at the Royal Naval College in Greenwich to mark his grandparent's fiftieth wedding anniversary. It was the first time they had all been together since the funeral, and Harry was especially glad to see his cousins again, particularly Peter Phillips.

When Christmas rolled around the following month, it was Peter who went out of his way to help Harry enjoy the holiday. With the loss of his mother still fresh, Harry found it difficult to embrace the spirit of the season at Sandringham. He was comforted, though, when he went to Crathie Kirk for Christmas services and heard his mother's name mentioned as the congregation prayed for her soul.

Turbulent, tragic 1997 came to an end.

As the new year got under way, Harry was

slowly but surely becoming his usual mischievous self again.

He had been infinitely amused when hundreds of giddy teenage girls showed up outside the November anniversary party for his grandparents—all of them screaming his brother's name. As William's heartthrob status became more and more apparent in the months that followed, Harry got a huge kick out of teasing him about it. He was especially good at mimicking the girls' lovesick shrieks and wails, and he did so at every opportunity.

Now that Diana's Kensington Palace apartment was no longer his home, Harry was going to be living with Prince Charles on the grounds at St. James's Palace. Their newly renovated five-bedroom home was located in historic York House.

The building, which has once been the home of King George V and Queen Mary, had most recently been home to the duke and duchess of Kent. It overlooks Cleveland Row, which is a public street, but is entered from the private Ambassadors Court in the palace itself. There, Harry was surrounded by his most cherished belongings, including keepsakes and framed photographs he had kept from his mother's Kensington Palace apartment.

In March 1998 Harry flew with his father to Canada for an official visit. William would be accompanying them, but he had to fly on a separate plane, chaperoned by Tiggy. Royal protocol strictly forbid the first two heirs to the throne, Charles and William, from taking the same flight in case of a crash.

In Vancouver the three Windsor men checked into a $1,200-a-night suite at the Waterfront Center Hotel. To make the boys' stay more pleasant, the management had stocked the room with chocolate and their favorite CDs by Savage Garden, Oasis, and The Spice Girls.

Outside the hotel, and everywhere they went, crowds of teenage girls gathered. The reluctant William was now one of the hottest heartthrobs on the planet, and Harry, too, had his share of admirers. While William was completely caught off guard and was mortified by all the female attention, Harry, true to character, grinned and enjoyed it.

At the Pacific Space Centre museum, Harry was thrilled to shoot off rockets, play computer games, and take a simulated trip to Mars. He and William teased each other good-naturedly as they played, like any pair of teenage brothers will do.

Afterward they made their way to a high

school in Burnaby, Harry smiling brightly for the cameras and thousands of fans who had gathered to greet them, while William ducked his head shyly. The boys were presented with caps and jackets from the Canadian Olympic team, which had recently been triumphant at the winter games, and they proudly wore them for the cameras.

A visit to Vancouver's waterfront Heritage Centre was meant to showcase Prince Charles, who was to give a speech. But the princes were the main attraction. Once again, William was the center of attention as hundreds of swooning girls screamed his name.

Harry, who also had girls calling him, begging to touch him, loved every minute of it. In true kid-brother fashion he started egging William on, directing him from one giddy group of females to another, cracking up merrily every time they went wild over his brother.

Harry, a renowned ski buff, was excited about the next leg of the trip, which was to be spent at Whistler, a resort an hour north of Vancouver. There he hit the snowy slopes, played hockey, and perfected his skills at his latest passion, snowboarding.

Naturally, he and William engaged in their usual good-natured competitiveness. When a reporter asked William if Harry lived up to his reputation as the family's best skier, William grinned and said, "I'm not sure about that."

The trip—the first the three Windsor males had taken alone together since Diana's funeral—was a huge success. Everywhere they went, they were met not just by passionate teenyboppers, but by smiling faces, applause, and on one occasion, a standing ovation when they merely walked into a café to eat lunch.

Back on home turf a few weeks later, Easter 1998 was spent at Balmoral. There, daredevil Harry was up to his old tricks, once again showing his exuberant, happy-go-lucky zest for living.

The fact that he was years away from being able to get his driver's license didn't stop him from sliding behind the wheel of his father's Range Rover. With his father and brother watching in amazement—and amusement—gutsy Harry zoomed up an icy slope in a move the royal bodyguards had said would be impossible.

During that break he also played host, inviting five favorite old friends to tea—namely, The Spice Girls.

Harry had not met them since the November introduction after their concert in South Africa. The previous December, he and William had attended the opening of the girls' new movie, *Spice*

World. Now the rock superstars, who were on tour, gladly accepted Harry's invitation to visit him at Highgrove.

The group flew to Gloucestershire by helicopter on a stormy afternoon and spent a few hours with Harry and Charles. Prince Charles was especially grateful for the support they had given to his Prince's Trust charity. Harry was the envy of teenage boys throughout the world.

Back in London later in the month, Harry went with Charles and William to see the popular Dame Edna Everage character onstage. During the show Dame Edna (Australian comic Barry Humphries in drag) commented on their presence in the audience and teased Harry and his brother about dressing up in women's clothing. Harry laughed hysterically at the notion, and so did Charles and William, who were finally taking Harry's cue and learning to enjoy themselves in public.

Both Diana and Charles had been concerned a year earlier about Harry's grades, and Diana was said to have been considering sending him to Radley College in Oxfordshire or Milton Abbey in Dorset.

Now Harry wanted only to be with William at Eton. During the first week in June, while still at Ludgrove, he sat for the difficult entrance exam, answering essay questions like "Briefly describe how a volcano is formed" and "Why did Charles I decide to rule without Parliament between 1629 and 1640?"

On June 10 St. James's Palace issued the triumphant statement: "The Prince of Wales is delighted with the news that Prince Harry has passed the Common Entrance Exam and has been accepted into Eton College next September. Prince Harry is thrilled."

It was a bittersweet victory—he knew how proud and thrilled his mother would have been by his accomplishment, and it hurt that she wasn't there to share it.

On Mother's Day Harry had sent flowers to Diana's grave. Now, during the last week of June, he went with William and Charles to visit the island site at the Spencer family estate. It was a private, sorrowful moment in a peaceful setting, away from cameras and probing eyes of strangers. Diana would have wanted it that way.

On July 1, her birthday, a museum was opened at Althorp to honor the memory of Diana, Princess of Wales.

Meanwhile, Harry and Charles had gone on to the World Cup Soccer match in Lens on June 26. Harry wore an English scarf to cheer on his team, and he was ecstatic when they beat Columbia

2–0. To his utter delight, after the game the players autographed a jersey for him, and he got to meet one of his soccer heroes, Sir Bobby Charlton.

Less than two weeks later, Charles and Harry appeared in public together again, this time at a royal charity stage performance of *Doctor Dolittle*. It was held at Labatt's Apollo in Hammersmith and featured dazzling Hollywood-style special effects. The musical-theater star Julie Andrews, show had provided a recorded voice for a character named Polynesia the Parrot, was seated with Harry and his father for the show.

Animal lover Harry was entranced by a menagerie of ninety-two electronic animals, including a snail, a seal, and a two-headed llama called a pushmi-pullyu that, to Harry's amusement, nearly bopped Prince Charles on the head with one of its humps.

That first summer without his mother marked another milestone in Harry's life—one that had been inevitable for some time. His father had continued to see Camilla Parker Bowles in the months since Diana's death. On June 12, William had bumped into her by accident at St. James's Palace, and had since had lunch and tea with her.

Now it was Harry's turn. His father introduced the two of them at a private lunch he hosted, and Harry later had tea alone with her. He did his best to accept the woman who had replaced his mother in his father's life, but it wasn't easy.

Harry was torn between wanting to like Camilla, since she had made his beloved father so happy, and resenting her for the misery she had caused Diana. In any case, the young prince had been trained well by both his parents. He used his manners, made polite conversation, and was relieved when the awkward first-time meeting was over.

Weeks later when Harry was happily back at Balmoral, he immersed himself in the rural sporting life he craved during the school year. But his legendary lust for adventure was about to land him in the papers—and in hot water with his father.

In the beginning of August, Tiggy brought Harry and William with her to visit her parents in Wales. At one point they stopped at Grwyne Fawr reservoir. The steep 160-foot dam—which holds back 400 million gallons of water—is a popular spot for abseilers, but all who participate in the sport must obtain a special permit and should use proper mountaineering equipment.

There, as Tiggy, his bodyguards, a few friends, and several tourists looked on, dauntless Harry donned a harness and scaled down the steep drop headfirst—without helmet, boots, or a backup safety rope. Photographs of his bold stunt appeared in the next day's newspapers, and

Charles was infuriated. He reprimanded Tiggy and the bodyguards severely for taking chances with his son's life.

Harry was scolded, too, of course, and he promised to be more careful in the future—not that it would be easy for a born daredevil to resist a challenge.

On August 31, Harry somberly marked the first anniversary of his mother's death with a private memorial service held at Crathie Kirk. Only the royal family, Prime Minister Tony Blair, and Blair's wife, Cherie, attended, again allowing Harry to mourn his beloved mother away from the curious gazes of strangers who meant well but nonetheless made his life more difficult. During the service, the Reverend Robert Sloan read Psalms 23 that begins "The Lord is My Shepherd," and verses 28 through 31 from Isaiah 40, "Comfort Ye My People Sayeth Your God."

Meanwhile, Harry was pleased that his grandmother, whose behavior had been so controversial—even hurtful—in the days after Diana's death, had ordered flags to fly at half-mast on all public buildings in Britain in honor of Diana.

He was far from the only one remembering his late mother on that melancholy anniversary. At Harrod's, a shrine was displayed in a store window, containing lit candles and photographs of

Diana and Dodi. An all-night candlelight vigil was held outside the gates of her former home, Kensington Palace. In Paris, at the crash site, people flocked to lay flowers. And at Althorp, where Diana was buried, the Spencer family had gathered for a simple, private ceremony.

And so the long and difficult year of mourning had come to an end. To mark its passing, Harry and William had their spokeswoman release a statement to the press on their behalf:

"Throughout the last year, since the death of their mother, Prince William and Prince Harry have been enormously comforted by the public sympathy and support they have been given; it has meant a great deal to them, and they have asked me to express their thanks once again to everyone. They have also asked me to say that they believe their mother would want people to now move on—because she would have known that constant reminders of her death can create nothing but pain to those she left behind. They therefore hope, very much, that their mother and her memory will now finally be allowed to rest in peace."

It was finally time to look to the future.

Time to allow grief to subside and to move on.

Time for a new beginning—one Harry had long anticipated.

Can You Speak Harry's Language?

While Prince Harry is enormously popular in his native land, he certainly has his share of fans in the United States. They might be crazy about the teenage prince, but they're most likely unfamiliar with British slang and colloquialisms. Although Harry speaks English, just as they do, his vocabulary is sprinkled with words and phrases that wouldn't necessarily spill from an American girl's lips.

Lots of kids in Britain use words that just haven't been included in the typical teenage vocabulary stateside for at least the past seventy-five years! Among them: *quite, indeed,* and *jolly.* Across the pond, teens might call a date *peculiar* or a test *frightful,* or say they're *mad about* chocolate. They might check the mirror and conclude that a new pair of jeans looks *smashing,* or inform their parents that they can't wait to go *to university* next year.

Sound foreign?

Not to worry. After all, when it comes to romance, there are no discrepancies in the world's most important way to communicate: body language.

Still, here's a handy-dandy guide to British slang so that if you ever meet Harry, and he invites you to *snog*, you'll jump at the chance!

Harry Might Say ...	Where You Would Say ...
"Excuse me, miss, do you play <u>football</u>?"	"I'm captain of my <u>soccer</u> team."
"It's <u>bloody</u> sweltering in here."	"Geez, why is it so <u>damn</u> hot?"
"What a <u>twit</u>."	"She's a complete <u>idiot</u>."
"Don't worry, she's just a <u>chum</u>."	"Him? No way! He's just my best <u>bud</u>."
"I'll <u>ring you up</u>."	"Here's my number, give me a <u>call</u>."
"He's behaving like an utter <u>prat</u>."	"Man, what a <u>jerk</u>!"
"Is there anything interesting on the <u>telly</u>?"	"No must-see tonight, just reruns. <u>TV</u> sucks."
"What are you doing <u>Boxing Day</u>?"	"On <u>the day after Christmas</u> I basically veg."

Harry Might Say . . .	Where You Would Say . . .
"That tabloid is filled with <u>rubbish</u>!"	"What a total pack of <u>lies</u>!"
"I'll just go put on my <u>jumper</u>."	"You might want to grab a <u>sweater</u>."
"We must <u>queue up</u>."	"Hey! Get <u>in</u> (or <u>on</u>) <u>line</u> like the rest of us!"
"Would you like a <u>crisp</u>?"	"Here, have a <u>chip</u>."
"Do you like fish and <u>chips</u>?"	"I could really go for a whopper with <u>fries</u>."
"Baby Spice and I are <u>muckers</u>."	"She's just your <u>friend</u>? Wow, that's a major relief."
"Where shall we go <u>on holiday</u>?"	"I'll go <u>on vacation</u> with you anywhere, anytime!"
"Would you like to <u>snog</u>?"	"Let's <u>make out</u>."

Harry Might Say . . .	Where You Would Say . . .
"I've finally been blooded."	. . . Er, okay, let's face it, sometimes the culture clash between the British aristocracy and the good old United States is just glaring. I mean, there is just no version of this in, say, suburban Chicago. But if there were, it would be: "Hey, congratulations! You must have shot your first stag, because someone put a big smear of fresh animal blood on your face and you're really pumped about it."

CHAPTER 9

Harry's Wilder Side

Two days after his mother's memorial service, on September 2, Harry and Charles drove to Windsor in a Vauxhall estate car. Unwilling to steal the spotlight from his little brother, William had stayed behind, allowing this to be Harry's shining moment. The thoughtful gesture spoke volumes about the tender, caring relationship between "the Heir" and "the Spare."

On the grounds of Eton, overlooking the Thames River, a smiling Harry emerged from the car wearing a light-green sport coat. He posed proudly for a mob of photographers and fans who had come to wish him well as he embarked on his new journey. The young prince waved cheerfully at everyone, appearing completely at ease in public once again—and thrilled to be the center of attention.

Of course his mother was on his mind. How Fiana would have loved to be there for him on that landmark occasion. All around Harry, the other boys' mothers were helping them settle in, giving them last-minute advice and voicing maternal worries.

Now Harry had only his father. But Prince Charles wholeheartedly stepped into Diana's role as he protectively and proudly escorted Harry into Manor House, his new dorm, for tea with Dr. Andrew Gailey, his new housemaster; Dr. Gailey's wife, Shauna, the house matron Elizabeth Heathcote, and several of his new schoolmates and their parents.

Later, Harry's feisty character was on full display as he prepared to fulfill a time-honored ritual and sign the school's entrance book. A few years earlier, William had accidentally put his name on the wrong line.

As Harry held the pen poised over the page, Prince Charles reminded him, "Make sure you sign it in the right place."

"Shut up, Dad," Harry promptly replied.

Unfazed, Charles watched Harry write his name, patted him on the back, and said affectionately, "Well done."

It was a moment that captured their relationship perfectly. Over the past year, Harry and his father had established a close, teasing relationship and discovered a mutual affection for each other. Harry, who had been accustomed to parental hugs and kisses while his mother was alive, didn't lack for affection now that she was gone.

In the years since Diana's death, Harry and Charles have frequently been photographed walking arm in arm or hand in hand. Harry sometimes covers his father's face with kisses until Charles laughingly begs him to stop.

After Charles had left Eton that first day, Harry went to his small ten-foot-by-seven-foot dorm room in the four-story ivy-covered Manor House. There, waiting for him, he found a regulation school kit and his brand-new made-to-measure uniform.

The room directly next door would be occupied by his full-time bodyguard. While he was living in the dorm Harry wouldn't have to make his own bed, clean his room, or do his laundry—all of those chores were handled by the maid. It wasn't a special privilege exclusively for Harry just because he was a prince. All boys at Eton are assigned maids, which provides some sense of just how exclusive a school it is.

There were about fifty other boys under the same roof, and they would all take their meals together there. They dressed alike in their distinct uniforms: black coats with tails, starched white shirts, ties, vests, pin-striped pants, and shiny black shoes. A former student, Chris Miller, recalls that it's difficult to walk in the strange uniform at first, and that "you can't really run at all, you have to learn to scuff your shoes along the floor to get up any speed."

British boarding schools, like American college frat houses, have their share of rituals—both official and unofficial. At Eton, one such tradition was to "lamp-post" the new boys. This meant creeping into their rooms while they were asleep, tying them across their middles to their beds, then standing the bed up abruptly, waking the instantly terrified victim.

If Harry was lamp-posted, his friends haven't revealed the incident publicly. In fact, to their credit, the vast majority of his schoolmates at Eton have been respectfully close-mouthed when it comes to discussing the young prince in their midst.

As Harry grew accustomed to life at his new school, he was exposed to a vast array of subjects. Here, in addition to the usual courses, he could learn everything from cooking to auto mechanics to Arabic. As for sports, he could indulge in some of his favorites: rugby, cricket, tennis, soccer, and rowing.

Harry was soon in his element out in the fresh air, romping with his classmates. Sometimes he walked into the small town of Windsor with them to visit the little shops or to grab a bite to eat—accompanied, of course, by his armed bodyguards.

Not long after he became a student at Eton, Harry and his new chums got into a scrape. Predictably, it landed in the tabloids. They had tried to copy the haircut of one of their heroes, soccer star Michael Owen—and wound up with disastrous results. To repair the damage, Harry had to visit a barber, whose only choice was to give him an ultra-short military-style cut.

The press had a field day. The *Mirror*'s cover headline read "HARRY THE SKINHEAD" and featured a computer-generated photo of the prince with a shaved head.

An uproar ensued. The *Mirror* claimed it had informed the palace of its intention to publish the story and photo, and that the palace had agreed it was amusing. The paper further claimed that it regularly refrained from publishing information about the princes and that just days earlier it had rejected a particularly provocative tidbit about Prince Harry on the grounds that it was an invasion of privacy.

Meanwhile, the palace retaliated. Prince Charles released a statement that read, "The story and computer-generated pictures in the *Daily Mirror* raise a general issue about the extent to which individual news stories about Prince

William and Prince Harry cumulatively constitute an intrusion into their privacy. It is a matter of considerable concern to the Prince of Wales, who will be raising the matter with the chairman of the Press Complaints Commission and industry's Code of Practice Committee."

Shortly after this, Harry and William made the journey from Windsor to Gloucestershire to celebrate Charles's fiftieth birthday on November 14. The party was hosted at Highgrove by Camilla— and the significance of this didn't escape the press. Nor did it escape the Queen and Prince Philip, who chose not to attend.

For the occasion, caterers had decorated the house with wildflowers, foliage, and Greek statues to duplicate Charles's beloved garden. Three hundred and forty of Charles's friends showed up, and it was a rousing affair.

Harry, with William, was in charge of the sound system. At one point, they played the old Village People hit "YMCA," clapping and stomping their feet as their father took the dance floor with Camilla.

Eventually Harry and William joined them there, bopping around in their elegant black tuxedos. Although they rolled their eyes in mock embarrassment at Charles's dance moves, it was clear to everyone that they were willing to welcome Camilla into their family.

While she lacks his mother's beauty and elegance, she is known as an easygoing, friendly woman, which appeals to upbeat, fun-loving Harry. Like him, she's down-to-earth, and she loves being outdoors in the country, even engaging in some of his favorite pursuits, like hunting and fishing. She's even reputed to be a bit sloppy in the way she dresses and keeps her house—Harry, whose mother often nagged him to clean up after himself, can relate to that.

Back at school Harry frequently wrote to his father. His style was warm and witty. When Charles was named an honorary rear admiral in the Royal Navy, Harry addressed a letter, "Rear Admiral Papa." He loved to decorate his letters with funny illustrations, and he was beginning to show an aptitude for art, with a natural talent for sketching and painting.

A week after his father's birthday party, Harry landed in the papers again. This time, the *Mirror* ran a story about a minor sports injury he had suffered. Charles was furious and publicly requested an apology. The *Mirror* responded with an accusation that the prince was trying to "bully and censor the press."

Charles fired back, "This matter is nothing at all to do with press freedom. Instead, it is everything to do with the privacy to which Harry and William are entitled during their education. It is about their ability to grow up without the telescope of publicity bearing down on their every move."

In a letter to Piers Morgan, the *Mirror's* editor, Charles pointed out that this was "the third trivial and intrusive story about Prince Harry since he started at Eton just two months ago. Despite your argument that the public has the right to know about the health of Prince Harry, I can assure you that there was absolutely no public interest whatever in the very minor bruising which Harry sustained—of the kind which can happen to children up and down the country on the playing field. Indeed, each of the stories you have run about him concerned events which happen to many other children. Yet you sensationalise them to an extent which makes it very difficult for Prince Harry to have a normal life at his school."

When the hubbub about Harry's press-related mishaps had died down, that Christmas at Sandringham was easier than the holiday the prior year. Now Harry was growing accustomed to life without his mother. While his grief still occasionally rose to the surface, it was becoming easier to remember only the good times, and to know she would have wanted him to enjoy life, even without her.

It was Harry who, with his father, led the family on foot from Sanringham house to the small white St. Mary Magdalen's Church. After the forty-minute service, he chatted with the crowd that had gathered in the rain. Then, with his family, he returned to the estate for lunch before settling down to watch the queen's annual Christmas broadcast at three o'clock.

A week later, Harry, Charles, Tiggy, and Harry's cousin Zara Phillips went to Klosters, the Swiss ski resort in the Alps. There, Harry and Charles agreed to a photo session with the press in exchange for being granted their privacy for the remainder of the trip.

Harry wore a stylish black ski suit over a red fleece pullover and on his head a black baseball cap he had bought the year before at Whistler. On short snowblades, without poles, Harry impressed the crowd with his expert jumps and left his father in the dust. "I suspect age—youth—has the advantage," Prince Charles said, beaming with pride and not seeming the least bit disappointed that his athletic son had outshone him.

On January 28, 1999, with Harry back at school, Charles and Camilla made their first public appearance as a couple. They attended a birthday party together for Camilla's sister Annabel Elliot at the Ritz Hotel in London.

Afterward, they braved a barrage of photographers camped out in front, smiling for the cameras and the cheering onlookers. Clearly, now that Harry and his brother had made it clear that they accepted their father's mistress, the British people were willing to follow suit.

Back at Eton for his second term, Harry was keeping up with his studies and enjoying the comradery of boarding-school life.

But tragedy struck on February 22 when a fifteen-year-old student, Nicholas Taylor, was found dead in his room. The boy had accidentally strangled himself with his bathrobe belt—apparently while playing a solo version of a dangerous game that was popular among the boys in the dorms. To play the game, two students would tie a cord around a willing third student's neck and pull it tighter and tighter until the victim passed out.

Nobody knows whether thrill-seeking Harry was ever involved in the game, but there was concern among the staff and the parents, not to mention at the palace, about the safety of the school's students. The tabloids were filled with the scandal, and Eton officials were especially vigilant following the tragedy.

Charles hadn't given up his battle to keep his sons out of the papers. On Thursday, April 29, new guidelines were issued by the Press Complaints Commission in response to Charles's issue with the *Mirror* after their coverage of Harry's haircut and his sports injury the previous fall.

The new rules specified that the press must respect Harry's privacy, along with William's, and use restraint when covering stories of interest to the public. After all, nobody could deny that the young princes were enormously popular both in Britain and abroad. Not only had they become international heartthrobs, but people around the world had taken a truly caring interest in the well-being of the two motherless boys.

PCC Chairman Lord Wakeham said, "The privacy of Prince William and Prince Harry continues to be of paramount importance and these new guidelines—based on the new, much tougher Code of Practice—are a practical and common-sense way to safeguard it. At the same time, it will ensure that newspapers will be able to chart their progress at school for their readers, among whom there is huge affection for these young men."

In keeping with that sentiment, the guidelines urged the palace to provide more stories about the princes, pointing out that the royals "will need to try to offer real stories about the princes, as well as photo opportunities. This, in turn, is likely to mean that fewer trivial, sensationalized stories actually appear: They themselves may be a symptom of a lack of genuine nonintrusive information. . . . At the same time, all newspapers should be aware of the problems posed by an accumulation of newspaper coverage of either of the royal princes ... [and] should seek a view about the likely impact of a particular story on one of the boys when assessing whether or not to publish a story. In doing so, editors should continue to err on the side of restraint as the code dictates that intrusions into a child's privacy should only be on a matter of exceptional public interest."

Harry breathed a sigh of relief when these new rules were released. It wasn't an ideal situation—he would, in a sense, be forced to cooperate with the press at times in exchange for privacy at other times. But ever since that grim September 1997 day when he greeted mourners outside Kensington Palace, he had been willing to do what was expected of him even when it violated his personal emotional needs. He could only hope that the media would live up to their end of the new bargain.

When another scandal connected to Charles hit the papers in mid-May, it didn't involve Harry or his brother. This time it was Tom Parker Bowles, Camilla's twenty-four-year-old son. He had admitted to using cocaine.

Tom, Charles's godson and a junior publicist with the Dennis Davidson Associates public relations firm, was someone Harry and William liked and had spent time with. He had even taken William out to nightclubs with him.

Now the papers were reporting that in addition to using drugs, he had been arrested for possession of marijuana and Ecstasy while he was a student at Oxford in 1995. The charges were eventually dropped and he claimed to have been clean ever since. Now Charles was concerned about the influence Tom might have had over William and Harry, and he lectured his sons sternly about the dangers of drugs.

A week later, on May 23, Harry watched his father play polo for his team, Acclaim Entertainment, in Surrey. Harry cheered when his father scored a goal. During breaks in the match, he stole the spotlight, playfully showing off for the ever-present cameras in a way that press-shy William never would have done.

Clad in khaki cargo pants, an open-collared blue button-down shirt, and a navy blazer with gold buttons, Harry entertained his father—and the photographers—with his mock karate moves. Then he grabbed hold of his father's polo mallet and pretended he wouldn't let go. Afterward, Charles, appearing moved by his son's affectionate playfulness and his ease in front of the crowds and cameras, seized him for a long, heartfelt hug that Harry returned. Obviously, father and son didn't care who was watching.

Photos of the exchange, including Harry's antics, were splashed all over newspapers and magazines. Harry, with his breezy self-confidence, had effortlessly charmed the press in much the same way as his mother might have done, and his laid-back, impish nature had rubbed off on Charles, who was far more relaxed in public with Harry than he had ever appeared to be on his own.

The summer of 1999 was filled with relaxation and contentment. By now the nightmare of the past had truly faded, and at last there were joyous times ahead for Harry.

The season was launched on Saturday, June 19, with an especially happy family occasion. That morning, Harry joined his family and 560 guests at St. George's Chapel, the setting for his own baptism fifteen years earlier. This time, the event was a wedding—smaller than that of Harry's parents almost two decades earlier, but a royal wedding just the same. It was televised to 200 million viewers around the world.

The groom was Prince Charles's youngest brother, Harry's uncle Edward. The bride was Sophie Rhys-Jones, a beautiful, personable blonde who was often compared to Princess Diana.

After the ceremony there was a lavish reception at Windsor Castle, complete with a towering cake made of chocolate fudge. Music was provided by the Royal Marines Band, which played oldies like "Mustang Sally" and "Delilah," and, of course, "YMCA"—which even the queen danced to, with Harry's cousins Beatrice and Eugenie. Harry and William mingled with their cousins and friends, and joined in line-dancing.

His first year of Eton successfully behind him, Harry vacationed in July with several of his friends in Cornwall by the sea. Photographers captured him clowning around on the side of a dock in a black wet suit, tossing one of his chums into the water and then dancing a triumphant barefoot jig on the wooden planks. Of course, moments later he was tossed overboard himself, and surfaced sputtering and grinning from ear to ear. Mischievous Harry was nothing if not a good sport.

On July 17, news from across the ocean brought viewers around the world to their television sets in an anxious vigil similar to the one that had been kept for Harry's mortally injured mum almost two years earlier.

An airplane piloted by thirty-eight-year-old John F. Kennedy Jr. was missing somewhere over the Atlantic, with the late president's son; his wife, Carolyn Bessette Kennedy; and her sister Lauren Bessette on board. Days later, the plane would be found on the bottom of the sea, along with three bodies.

The tragedy rocked the world the way Diana's death had. The Kennedys have been called

America's version of the British royal family, and Diana had considered JFK Jr. a role model for Harry and William. She often said that she admired the way he had grown up to be a solid, happy man, seemingly unaffected by life in the spotlight or the tragedies of his family's past.

There are striking similarities between Prince Harry and JFK Jr. Both were famous long before they entered the world, and their births were greeted with worldwide celebration and massive press coverage. Arguably the world's most famous kid brothers, Harry and JFK Jr. were born to high-profile parents in troubled marriages, both to adulterous fathers and glamorous mothers who were adored as much for their fashion trendsetting as they were for their maternal skills as they raised young children in the constant glare of cameras.

Like Harry, JFK Jr. was a gifted athlete with a bit of cocky daredevil in his blood. He, too, was more happy-go-lucky than his older sibling. He, too, attended the finest private schools and struggled with his grades at times. Both lived amidst the trappings of great wealth, yet thanks to qualities instilled in them by their mothers, they somehow managed to stay down-to-earth and come across as "regular guys."

Perhaps the most tragic bond between England's "Spare" and America's "Hunk" is that they both lost a beloved young parent at an early age, violently and completely unexpectedly. Both faced their losses within days of their birthdays, forever casting a shadow over the celebrations of the yearly milestone. Both were forced to mourn in public and to endure ongoing speculation about, and investigations into, the circumstances surrounding the deaths.

And, most poignantly, in their sorrow, both unwittingly created haunting images that would become somber symbols of their parents' funerals: JFK Jr. saluting his father's coffin; Prince Harry walking, head bowed, behind his mother's.

As much as he took his fame in stride, JFK Jr., like Diana, was a victim of it in the end. He had taken to flying his own plane because he disliked the hassles of commercial airline travel. Everywhere he went, he was recognized and stalked by tabloid photographers, increasingly so in the years after he married Carolyn Bessette. As a pilot, he could escape all that—soar away from the relentless press in a way Diana herself had often longed to do.

For Harry, JFK Jr.'s death was a grim reminder of the ordeal that was never far from his mind. Yet he was determined, as always, not to dwell on the tragedies to which no one—not even the globe's most privileged citizens—is immune.

Things settled back to normal. On the last

weekend in July, Harry was at Highgrove with his father and William, who was learning to drive. Clad in corduroys, an open-neck dress shirt under a navy sweater, and boating shoes, he posed with his father and brother for an official photo op to satisfy the press so that they would be left alone by the media to enjoy the rest of their vacation.

During the session, William showed off his driving skills in a silver Ford Focus with his Metropolitan Police driving instructor at his side. Charles had given him a brand-new sports car for his birthday a month earlier, and Harry was looking forward to the day his brother got his license so that the two of them could take off together.

The reporters on hand couldn't help noticing that Harry had shot up, and while he hadn't yet overtaken William's six-foot height, had clearly caught up to his father's. Charles, standing between Harry and William, quipped, "This is just to show how quickly I'm shrinking."

On Tuesday, August 3, Harry once again proved that he was just a regular, good-natured guy—and this time, the whole world found out about his generous spirit. As he was riding along a road in the Chelsea section of London with William and some friends, he spotted a broken-down BMW and two men trying to push it.

The car belonged to software salesman Simon

Thompson, and he was being assisted by an off-duty police officer named Steven James. The two were shocked when a green SUV pulled up and Prince Harry popped out of the backseat.

He hurried over to lend a hand pushing the car off the road, followed by Prince William, who pitched in beside him.

"They acted as thought it was no big deal," Thompson said. "I could not look them in the face because I did not want them to feel uncomfortable, but it is amazing when there are two princes pushing your car down the road."

After performing his good deed, Harry hopped back into his car with William and they drove off, unaware that the men they had helped were completely stunned—and impressed—by their actions. They alerted the press, who proudly hailed Harry and William's impromptu rescue mission and proclaimed them heroes.

The following day, the carrottopped Good Samaritan joined his great-grandmother, the Queen Mother, in celebrating her ninety-ninth birthday at her official London residence, Clarence House. Harry, clad in a suit and tie despite the summer heat, joined his great-grandmother in greeting the crowds that had gathered at the gate. Naturally, teenage girls went wild at the sight of him and William. Following a forty-one-gun salute fired by the King's Troop Royal Horse Artillery—

which had saluted Harry on the day he was born—he joined his family inside for lunch.

Immediately afterward, he flew to Athens, Greece, with his father to embark on an eleven-day vacation. Joining them, in addition to William and reportedly at William's suggestion, were Camilla Parker Bowles and her two children, twenty-year-old Laura and twenty-four-year-old Tom. It was the first time Harry and William had ever traveled with Camilla.

Trailed by the press, the group boarded the *Alexander*, a luxury yacht owned by shipping magnate Yannis Latsis, and they embarked on a cruise of the Greek Islands along the sparkling waters of the Aegean Sea. In a repeat scenario of Harry's vacation with his mother in the Mediterranean two years earlier, they were hounded by photographers in boats and helicopters, including BBC, Reuters, and Associated Press reporters disguised as tourists.

But in the wake of their mother's death, the Press Commission's Code specified that photos snapped of Harry and William could not be printed without Charles's consent "unless there is exceptional public interest."

A little more than two years after Diana's death, the investigation into the fatal Paris car accident came to a close. On September 3, French magistrates Herve Stephan and Marie-Christine

Devidal ruled that the crash was caused by drunk driving. Despite the paparazzi's role in the tragedy, the bottom line was that Henri Paul, the Ritz employee who was at the wheel of the car, had more than three times the legal limit of alcohol in his blood. The finding was appealed by Henri Paul's family and by Dodi's father, Mohamed Al Fayed, who, as owner of the Ritz and therefore Paul's employer, faced numerous lawsuits.

On the Friday the news was released, Harry and William were no longer at Balmoral where they had spent their usual August vacation after returning from the Greek cruise. Now they were back in England with Charles. The three of them, father and sons, were contentedly engaged in watching a new air assault brigade in Suffolk, and didn't publicly acknowledge the French court's ruling.

Days later, Harry was back at Eton to start his second year. On September 15, he celebrated his fifteenth birthday.

In the months that followed, as the year 1999 wound to a close, he was surrounded by his cherished brother and father, his loyal school chums, and a family that had weathered its share of storms.

As usual, Tiggy was there for him when he needed her, and Harry knew that she always would be. But Harry and William were no longer the only men in their nanny's life. On October 15, Harry climbed into a car with William at the wheel, and the two brothers journeyed to the 6,000-acre Legge-Bourke riverside estate near Crickhowell in Wales.

There, the following day, in a small church located on the grounds, they watched thirty-four-year-old Tiggy exchange wedding vows with former Coldstream Guard Charles Pettifer. The event was celebrated with champagne and canapes on a sprawling lawn, followed by a gala reception under a tent.

Harry was truly happy that Tiggy had found a Prince Charming of her own. Now she had two stepchildren who would keep her busy, although she would of course continue to make time for Harry and Wills. Harry would never forget how she had gotten him through the two most difficult times of his life. Now, at fifteen, he was ready to go it alone.

Harry spent the last Christmas of the century steeped, as always, in Windsor tradition. He celebrated at Sandringham with his father and the rest of the royal family, as he had every December of his life. On Christmas Eve he gathered with them around the huge tree and opened presents. In their long-standing habit, the family who had everything exchanged only silly gag gifts with each other.

On Christmas Day, Harry joined the rest of the Windsors at services at St. Mary Magdalen Church. William was under the weather and stayed home that day, having gone to bed early the night before.

At some point during that holiday season at Balmoral, carrottopped Harry and his older brother visited another famous royal redhead—their aunt, Sarah Ferguson. Beatrice and Eugenie's mother was, as Diana had been, banished from attending the holiday festivities at Sandringham following her divorce from Prince Andrew. However, she was allowed to stay at a cottage on the grounds to be near her daughters.

Sarah, who had been a great friend of Harry's mother during much of Diana and Charles's marriage, had spent lots of time with them as they were growing up. Her divorce and the media uproar over her "scandalous" behavior (among her crimes: she had written her autobiography and had become a spokeswoman for Weight Watchers) had resulted in Fergie's being treated as a royal outcast despite the fact that she was the mother of the two young princesses.

Sarah had recently told a reporter that she deeply missed her nephews and hadn't been allowed to see them. In visiting her, Harry showed that he might have Windsor blood in his veins, but his mother's influence hadn't faded. Like Diana, he was willing to show his humanity, and to stand up for what he believed was right—even in the face of intense scrutiny by the elder royals. His mother had done her job well, accomplishing the maternal mission that had driven her from the time she gave birth to "the Heir" and "the Spare."

On New Year's Eve, Harry reportedly rang in Y2K with William in Norfolk, joined at a private party by his aunt Jane's daughter Laura Fellowes and several of their friends.

The next day, he joined his father in Wales for a lively church service at the Tabernacle Baptist Church in Cardiff. The weather was cold and rainy, but Harry spent ten minutes outside the church shaking hands with the large crowd that had gathered. As always, he cheerfully clasped the hands of besotted girls who had waited hours in the nasty climate just to see him, rewarding them with his famous broad grin.

Later, he went on with his father and William to a special celebration at Cardiff's Millennium Stadium. More than 66,000 people had gathered there for the BBC's Songs of Praise broadcast. The concert included a choir of 5,000 voices and a 100-harp orchestra, and recording star Sir Cliff

Richard performed his hit song "Millennium Prayer."

Meanwhile, a fresh scandal was brewing back home. On that first day of the new century, Harry's eighteen-year-old cousin, Nicholas Knatchbull, the great-grandson of his late great-uncle Earl Mountbatten, was arrested for speeding. The passengers in his car were also arrested, on drug possession charges. The press descended like vultures.

No matter.

For the rest of Harry's life, rpyal scandals—along with tragedies and celebrations—will come and go. If the past is any indication, the happy-go-lucky prince will continue to sail past them, guided by a loving father who provides steadfast support—and the lasting lessons taught by a mother whose spirit lives on in the son she adored.

The once elfin, freckle-faced little boy has become long and lanky; his famous strawberry hair is close-cropped above his ears, yet it often appears boyishly tousled. He has inherited his mother's good looks and her way with people, easily charming strangers with his effortless grin and twinkling blue eyes. He has his father's grounded personality, taking in stride all the perks and drawbacks that come with life in the public eye, and is strongly aware of the responsibility he bears to the monarchy and to his country.

When he isn't at school or traveling, Harry is with his father at Highgrove or at the large apartment Charles had renovated at St. James's Palace, York House in London. While William now has his own apartment there, Harry still stays with his father, to whom he is as close as ever.

Harry and William continue to get along very well, and are each other's closest confidants. They still display a healthy competitive spirit, especially in athletics. When Harry and William ventured on to the polo field at Cirencester Park Polo Club last year, they played on opposing teams. William played for his father's former team, the Lovelocks, positioned as an attacker at Number One. Harry, meanwhile, playing for Spiral, was in a defensive position at Number Four, which was his father's usual number and position. Since Number Four always pairs off with the opposing team's Number One, William and Harry were able to engage in some brotherly aggression for the sake of the match.

But their days together are coming to an official end, now that William has left Eton behind to embark on a university career—and, eventually, the throne he was born to inherit.

As for Harry, he'll stay on at Eton for the time being, toiling to keep his grades up.

There's no telling what he'll do with his future. Unlike William, he'll have some say in the matter.

Perhaps the boy who was fascinated by toy soldiers as a child will grow up to become a military officer. Or maybe he'll represent England in the Olympics, as his equestriene aunt, Princess Anne, once did. He might even become a professional athlete. Or an artist.

Time will tell.

Yet one thing is fairly certain. Now that Harry, like his older brother, receives bags full of love letters from smitten girls, there's no doubt that he'll at some point turn his attention to romance. He won't face the pressure that William will endure—and his father did before him—to marry a certain kind of person, a female who fits the royal image. Harry will be free to marry the woman he chooses, and for one reason alone: love.

The girl who captures his heart will undoubtedly be independent and fun-loving, athletic and witty, playful and affectionate, and most importantly of all, head over heels in love with her prince.

And who wouldn't be?

Lovable Harry has it all—good looks, wealth; tons of personality; a kind, caring nature; an ability to make people smile.

His Royal Highness Prince Henry Charles Albert David Windsor might never rule the land, but like his mother, the boy known as Harry is guaranteed to rule where it counts the most: in people's hearts.

Harry or William? The Debate Rages On!

As the twentieth century gives way to the twenty-first, the Internet has become a well-traveled forum for fans of Britain's teenage princes. Some can't decide which one of Di and Charles's sons they prefer. For others, the choice is obvious. Here are some Web site comments from adoring females who have determined that second-born Harry will never be second-best:

"Harry is more optimistic tham William. He would be the type of person who would be the life of the party. I like to have a lot of fun and Harry is the type of person who could help you do that."—Karri

"Harry is so much cuter than William. He has a much better personality and his ears are adorable."—Erin

"He is just as important as Wills is. And I like him for who he is inside . . . not for his money or looks or anything like that."—Angela

"I live in London. . . . After their mother died . . . I got to shake Harry's hand. He was very kind and thanked me for coming out. When William came around he just smiled and wasn't anxious to interact with people like Harry was."—Mollie

"I think Harry looks like he WANTS to be your friend. He looks very huggable, too!!=) Anytime that bad stuff happens like rumours and other stuff, I always just want to give him a hug!"—Halie

"I am not British, but I still like Harry. He seems more like an American because he is laid back and likes to have fun and I think that's cool."—Allison

"Harry is HOT. He seems super nice, too."—Lola

"I like Harry because he is a strong person. I have heard that he is very nice and funny. I thought the stories about him being a mischievous little boy were cute."—Dalia

Prince Harry Trivia Quiz

Give yourself one point for every correct answer; subtract one point for every wrong answer.

1. What is Prince Harry's full titled name? (Make sure you get the right order or it doesn't count!)

2. Name the date and year Prince Harry was born. Add one Bonus Point if you know the time of day!

3. What was Princess Diana's maiden name?

4. What is the name of the estate where the royals spend Christmas every year?

5. Where did Prince Harry continue his education after he finished nursery school at Mrs. Mynor's?

6. During which year, the famed *"annus horribilis,"* did Harry's parents announce their separation?

7. In which London palace did Harry share an apartment with his mother and brother?

8. Where did Harry spend his last vacation with his mother during the summer of 1997?

9. Where was Harry when he got the news about his mother's fatal car crash?

10. What is the name of Harry's Eton dorm?

Answers:

1. His Royal Highness, Prince Henry Charles Albert David Windsor
2. September 15, 1984, at 4:20 P.M.
3. Spencer
4. Sandringham
5. Wetherby School
6. 1992
7. Kensington Palace
8. Saint Tropez
9. At Balmoral Castle in Scotland
10. Manor House

SCORING

10–11: *Excellent*
Congratulations! You're well-prepared for the day Harry, on a walkabout, spots you in the crowd, your eyes lock, and . . . bliss!

7–9: *Very Good*
When it comes to Harry, few details escape you. You've done your homework—someday,

with luck, you'll get to put your knowledge to good use!

4–6: *Fair*

Not bad, but if you want to stand a chance with the prince of your dreams, you'd be wise to get to know him a little better.

1–3: *Uh-oh*

Better turn back to page one and start rereading! After all, you never know when and where you might bump into huggable Harry.

About the Author

Wendy Brody lives with her family in New York. She is the author of many novels under a variety of pseudonyms, including young adult horror and romance, as well as suspense, mystery and romance for adult readers. Wendy loves to hear from readers and you may write to her c/o Pinnacle Books. Please include a self-addressed stamped envelope if you wish a response.